Becoming a

RESONANT
LEADER

Becoming a

RESONANT LEADER

DEVELOP *Your Emotional Intelligence*

RENEW *Your Relationships*

SUSTAIN *Your Effectiveness*

Annie
McKEE

Richard
BOYATZIS

Frances
JOHNSTON

Harvard Business Press
Boston, Massachusetts

Library of Congress Cataloging-in-Publication Data

McKee, Annie, 1955–
    Becoming a resonant leader: develop your emotional intelligence, renew your
relationships, sustain your effectiveness / Annie McKee, Richard Boyatzis, and
Frances Johnston.
        p. cm.
    ISBN 978-1-4221-1734-7 (perm. paper)
    1. Leadership—Psychological aspects. 2. Emotional intelligence.
3. Interorganizational relations 4. Organizational effectiveness. 5. Teams in the
workplace—Management. I. Boyatzis, Richard E. II. Johnston, Frances, 1964–
III. Title.
  HD57.7.M3958 2008
  658.4'092—dc22

                                                                    2007036568

The paper used in this publication meets the requirements of the American
National Standard for Permanence of Paper for Publications and Documents
in Libraries and Archives Z39.48-1992.

We dedicate this book to

our children's hopes and dreams.

Rebecca Renio

Sean Renio

Sarah Renio

Andrew Murphy

Mark Scott

Lucas Johnston-Peck

Miguelangel Johnston-Peck

Contents

Preface and Acknowledgments   ix

1. Leading for Real   1
    Becoming the Leader You Most Want to Be

2. Resonant Leadership   11
    What It Takes

3. Listening to Your Wake Up Calls   45
    Staying Awake, Aware, and Ready to Learn

4. Seeing Your Dream   69
    Building an Energizing Personal Vision

5. Appreciating Your Real Self   109
    Seeing the Whole Picture

6   Becoming a Resonant Leader   151
    Taking Your Desires from Awareness into Action

7. Igniting Resonance   175
    *Creating Effectiveness in Teams, Organizations,
    and Communities*

Notes   215
List of Exercises   225
Index   227
About the Authors   231

Preface and Acknowledgments

We have been studying leadership for many years and are often asked why we think it is so important. To us, there is no nobler goal than to lead people to excellence, fulfillment, and collective achievement. Our lives, our society, and our planet have changed rapidly and unpredictably in recent years—and this is probably just the tip of the iceberg. If we are to find our way to a better world, a more stable environment, and societies in which all people have access to life's gifts, we need people who can see beyond today, spark hope instead of despair, and draw others into an intentional journey of transformation. We need more great leaders who think and act in new ways—women and men unafraid to travel the road less taken, the road that requires vision and courage.

The capacity to mobilize energy toward improving the quality of people's lives is one of the most fascinating and crucial abilities to understand—and, ultimately, to master. Throughout our research, practice, and writing, we've sought to answer these questions: What is great leadership? What differentiates the best leaders from the average? How can people improve their capacity for resonant leadership, and how can they sustain effectiveness in the face of the daunting responsibilities and inevitable challenges of their roles?

In 2002 we wrote *Primal Leadership* with Daniel Goleman to begin to answer these questions. We shared research, stories, and our own experiences to build the case that emotional intelligence and the ability to create resonant relationships were the keys to great leadership. But one question persisted: why do so many good leaders fail to reach their potential?

In *Resonant Leadership*, we again shared research and stories that show how even the best leaders can find it difficult to sustain effectiveness over time. This is, ironically, particularly true for good leaders—people who take their roles and responsibilities seriously. In that book, we explained why people often lose their capacity for resonance—they get caught in the Sacrifice Syndrome. We also showed how leaders can avoid this syndrome when they adopt practices that spark renewal: mindfulness, hope, and compassion. By tapping into mindfulness and cultivating the capacity for hope and compassion, leaders manage the cycle of sacrifice and renewal while sustaining resonance and effectiveness over time.

As the messages of these books have spread, we have been asked by people around the world, *How* can I create resonant relationships? *How* can I develop emotional intelligence and resonant leadership? *How* can I renew myself and return to resonance?

We have written this book to answer these questions. We have summarized our key ideas, as well as the research, and included stories of leaders who have managed to develop and sustain resonance. We have also taken a deliberate departure from our previous books' approaches. This book includes the most powerful and transformative exercises that we have used with leaders across the globe in all types of organizations. These exercises will help you develop emotional intelligence and your capacity for resonant leadership as you chart a path toward your personal vision for your life and work. We encourage you to really *use* this book—as you would a workbook. In other words, *write in it* as you move through the chapters and as you work toward the goal of creating and sustaining resonant leadership—whether you wish to renew this quality in yourself or to inspire it in others around you.

The Best Way to Use This Book

This book is a tool for personal and professional growth. We want our concepts and exercises to be useful to you. And, because this book is probably quite different from other leadership and self-development books you may have read, we would like to prepare you to work most effectively with the ideas and exercises.

Below are a few tips that we have developed from years of experience with the ideas, research, and exercises. Following the list of tips for using the book is a detailed outline that shows you what lies ahead.

Tips for Getting the Most from This Book

- ***Do the exercises.*** It is the only way to apply the concepts in the book.

- ***Take time to reflect.*** The exercises are best done one, two, or, at most, three in one sitting. Do a few, and then come back to the concepts and next exercises later—this pace will give you some time to digest what you've learned so that each sitting allows you to build on the previous ones. Going too quickly through the exercises often results in missing some of the most useful and transformative experiences for leaders.

- ***Think and feel as you go.*** Progress requires reflection—this means thinking and noticing your feelings about the concepts and insights you develop from the exercises.

- ***Consider working with a partner.*** Often, people find that talking with trusted others helps them extract more insight from the thoughts and feelings evoked by the exercises.

- ***Don't be in a rush.*** It took you years (or decades) to get to this point. You will not find a desired path to the future in a few minutes or even a few hours. Give yourself the gift of time.

- *Realize that people are different.* At times we offer exercises that might overlap in helping you craft your vision for a desired future and your plan to get there. We do not know which exercise will work best for you. So if you have achieved tremendous insight from a few exercises, and are reading another that seems similar, you may spend a little less time on it. But remember, each exercise has a distinct purpose and is tied carefully to those that come before and after. It is best to try to do them all, and in order.

- *Pay attention to how, when, and where you use this book.* If you are like most busy professionals, you will probably try to fit this book into your time on planes, at the end of the day, and so forth. We suggest that you also give yourself the gift of dedicated time when you are refreshed and sharp. Sit in a comfortable, inspiring place if you can. Treat the reading of this book and your completion of the exercises as important work—work that requires concentration and inspiration.

The Journey to Resonant Leadership

As we have just suggested, your path to resonant leadership can be smoother if you follow the sequential route reflected in the order of the chapters. After setting up our main ideas and our approach to leadership and learning in chapter 1, we start in chapter 2 by reflecting on what, exactly, it takes to be a *resonant leader.* A few exercises will help you consider who depends on you for guidance and inspiration, and *how you lead* people. We will also share exercises, stories, and our research about what great leaders think, feel, and do. You will learn some common myths about leadership, the importance of emotional and social intelligence, and how good leaders manage the pressure and inevitable sacrifices of their roles through mindfulness, hope, compassion, and renewal.

In chapter 3, we will share how to build your capacity for *mindfulness*. Some people use life's laboratory to learn and grow constantly—they are awake, aware, and attuned to themselves, others, and the environment. But because even great leaders lose their way sometimes, we will explore *wake-up calls*—the messages that tell you that you are heading in the wrong direction.

In chapter 4, we will focus on the foundation of your leadership: your strengths, your values, and the sense of purpose and meaning that fuels your desire to be a great leader and a great person. The outcome of this chapter is a personal, meaningful vision of yourself and your future—this is your *Ideal Self* and your desired future.

In chapter 5, we will enable you to look at who you are now, as a leader and as a person. This is your *Real Self*: Which of your strengths support your vision of the future? What roles do you enjoy, and which of these provide meaning for you? What life experiences have shaped who you are? Finally, what might you need to change or do to bridge the gaps between where you are today and where you want to be in the coming months or years? Doing the exercises in chapter 5 will give you a deep sense of yourself; this self-awareness is essential for effective leadership.

In chapter 6, you will pull all your learning together to craft a plan for *Intentional Change*. Because the press of day-to-day work short-circuits many people's natural desire to grow, development doesn't just happen—you need conscious effort. Your plan for change will help you focus your energy and time on making your dreams come true.

In chapter 7, we will look at what it takes to create resonance in a group. We will present a few lessons on how to build a shared vision and engage people in collective action. You might use this process to create resonance with your team: the people you lead and with whom you work most closely. You may even decide to apply this process to a larger group—your organization or community.

Finally, as you finish chapter 7, you will see that the end of this book is really the beginning of your journey. The journey propels you toward a meaningful future and resonant leadership through which you can have impact on the people and world around you in very positive ways.

Acknowledgments

With gratitude and respect we acknowledge the many people who have dedicated themselves to pursuing their dreams and becoming great leaders. You—our colleagues, friends, students, and clients—have purposefully and successfully developed resonant leadership in yourselves and in those around you. We thank you for sharing yourselves with us in the pursuit of knowledge and our dreams for ourselves, our institutions, and our communities.

Several dear colleagues have had particular impact on us and on this book. For your commitment, creativity, and courage, we thank Kleio Akrivou, Juan Manuel Battista, Marco Bertola, Sharon Brownfield, Ron Cheeley, Michelle Conlin, Carroll Connacher, Matt Doherty, Kirstin von Donop, Kirsten Dunlop, Monsignor Vladimir Felzman, Ingrid FitzGerald, Niall FitzGerald, Tom Glocer, Darren Goode, Fred Graff, Hope Greenfield, Laura Guillen, Vic Gulas, Fred Hassan, Margaret (Miggy) Hopkins, Anita Howard, Maryann Kraus, Severine Leonardi, Tony Lingham, Ken Lombard, Metsi Makhetha, Michael Markovits, Jennifer Milwee, Vas Nair, Mark Newton, Roberto Nicastro, Allesandro Profumo, Betsy Redfern, Ricard Serlavos, Monica Sharma, Melvin Smith, Dan Sontag, John Studzinski, Bill Tate, Lechesa Tsenoli, Ellen Van Oosten, C. J. Warner, Connie Wayne, Scott Whelehan, and Elizabeth Wood.

We are fortunate to work closely with people who dedicate their lives to learning about great leadership and designing practices that actually support others in reaching their dreams. Each of these people is special in his or her own right—the world is lucky to have you:

Teleos Leadership Institute: Eddy Mwelwa, Laura Peck, Barbara Dávila, Adriene Hobdy, Delores Mason, Bobbie Nash, Toby Nash, Matthew Ochs, Suzanne Rotondo, David Smith, Felice Tilin, Christina Yerkes, and Amy Yoggev. Additional thanks to Teleos Associates Laura Mari i Barrajón, Alberto Castigliano, Rob Emmerling, Cordula Gibson, Jeff Kaplan, Hilary Lines, Jochen Lohmeier, Gianluca Lotti, Bob McDowell, Michael McElhenie, Nosisa Mdutshane, Linda Pittari, Gretchen Schmelzer, Marinella Soldi, Sander Tideman, Beulah Trey, and Chantelle Wyley.

The Weatherhead School of Management, Case Western Reserve University, Department of Organizational Behavior: David Aron, Diana Bilimoria, Terrence Brizz, Aleece Carron, Susan Case, David Cooperrider, Loren Dyck, Ron Fry, Lindsey Godwin, David Kolb, Mihaly Maserovic, Eric Neilsen, Deborah O'Neil, Patricia Petty, Sandy Piderit, Brigette Rapisarda, Beatriz Rivera, Melvin Smith, Danny Solow, Betty Vandenbosch, and Helen Williams.

ESADE: Jaume Hugas, Carlos Losada, Xavier Mendoza, Ricard Serlavos, and Ceferi Soler.

Inspirational colleagues: James Bailey (George Washington University), Arnauldo Comuffo (Bocconi), Jane Dutton (University of Michigan), Olga Epitropaki (ALBA Athens), Cary Cherniss (Rutgers University), Dennis Encarnation (Harvard University), Lynda Gratton (London Business School), Margaret Hopkins (University of Toledo), John Kotter (Harvard University), Kathy Kram (Boston University), Peter Kuriloff (University of Pennsylvania), Babis Mainemelis (London Business School), Tom Malnight (IMD), Janet Patti (Hunter College), Ken Rhee (University of Northern Kentucky), Greg Shea (The Wharton School), Kenwyn Smith (University of Pennsylvania), Robert Stern (Columbia University), Scott Taylor (Boston University), Susan Wheelan (Temple University), and Jane Wheeler (Bowling Green State University).

And finally, thanks and love to one more special colleague: Daniel Goleman. He is truly an inspiration to us and to the millions of people he touches.

Special and abiding thanks to all of the great people who have supported us as we wrote this book. Our editor, Jeff Kehoe, continues to guide us with grace, humor, and brilliance. The team at the Press is outstanding. Each person who touched us and this book has been fantastic. Hollis Heimboch leads a resonant team of true professionals—all are fun to work with. Particular thanks to those closest to us and to the project: Liz Baldwin, Marcy Barnes-Henrie, Todd Berman, Mark Bloomfield, Erin Brown, Stephani Finks, Ralph Fowler, David Goehring, Sarah Green, Daisy Hutton, Sarah Mann, Carolyn Monaco, Zeenat Potia, Christine Turnier-Vallecillo, and Leslie Zheutlin.

In addition to the core team at the Press, Terry Irwin's magical touch has made all the difference in how this book looks and feels. Thank you!

Very special thanks to Teleos team members Delores Mason, Suzanne Rotondo, Amy Yoggev, and Christina Yerkes. All of them care passionately about this project and contributed the best of themselves to ensure that this book reached the high standards we share. They read every page numerous times, contributed creatively, and kept us on track and in sync. Their belief in the value of this work, and their intelligence and good humor are a delight.

Many people have supported us behind the scenes, including Richard Alston, Mary Ann Batos, Sarah Drazectic, Bob Freedman, Cindy Frick, Andrea Jung, Doug Lennick, Ruth Malloy, Erato Paraschaki, Franco Ratti, Fabio Sala, Lyle Spencer, Bernhard Urs, and Steve Wolff. Special thanks to Carlton Sedgeley and the team at Royce Carlton for helping us to find venues to share our messages around the world.

We wish to thank our children and our families. They've been with us every step of the way: Murray Wigsten; Rebecca, Sean, and Sarah Renio; Andrew Murphy; Rick, Matt, Mark, Rob, Jeff, and Sam Wigsten; Mark Scott; Hugh, Suzanne, Claire, and Huguette Johnston; and Lucas and Miguelangel Johnston-Peck.

And finally, deep love and immeasurable gratitude to our partners: Eddy Mwelwa, Sandy Boyatzis, and Laura Peck. In these relationships, we are blessed to experience resonance and find support for pursuit of our ideals.

We welcome correspondence from our readers, and look forward to hearing from many of you through e-mail: amckee@teleosleaders.com; richard.boyatzis@case.edu; fjohnston@teleosleaders.com; or through our Web sites, www.teleosleaders.com and www.weatherhead.case.edu.

Chapter 1

LEADING FOR REAL

Becoming the Leader You Most Want to Be

THIS BOOK CHARTS A JOURNEY for your transformation as a leader. In these pages, you will find inspiration, information, and practical activities to help you become the leader you most want to be. As you read and reflect, you will have a chance to wrestle with profound aspects of yourself as a person and as a leader so that you can become more resonant, develop your emotional intelligence, renew your relationships, and sustain your effectiveness.

We will review the research and state-of-the-art leadership practices in a straightforward and no-nonsense way to give you a solid grounding in proven methodologies, rather than a sampling of leadership "flavors of the month." We will also share kernels of wisdom discovered on our personal leadership journeys and through our work with some of the world's best (and worst) leaders, who range from A-level college basketball coaches to CEOs of *Fortune* 100 companies to people like you—accomplished and dedicated professionals. Through their stories, you will hear about very difficult and sometimes very public personal trials and successes. Ultimately, you will see how the best leaders get results by courageously striving to become the best *people* they can be, while making decisions that ensure a viable future for the individuals, organizations, and countries they lead.

Becoming and sustaining resonant leadership isn't always easy; you may feel personally challenged as you read and work through the exercises in this book. If that is the case, you're on the right track. Being a great leader can be deeply rewarding at work and in life. Sustaining it requires a deep dive into your hopes, dreams, fears, and sorrows. But be assured that when you master the art of resonant leadership, you will be on the road to mastering the art of living as well.

People who consciously reach for a dream of a better future for themselves and others tend to live full, passionate, and meaningful lives. They build—and sustain—powerful and positive relationships at work and at home. These leaders find excitement in life's challenges and, with patience, strength, and serenity, meet the trials, the loss, and the inevitable disappointments we all have.

Resonant leaders embrace today's challenges and tomorrow's promise. They are unflagging in their commitment to personal values, without being locked into narrow-minded or narcissistic ways of viewing the world. Such leaders face reality with courage and creativity. Resonant leaders live and lead with hope and optimism. They capture passion—their own and that of others—and use emotion, relationships, and vision to move people toward a better future.[1]

Resonant leaders are attuned to themselves and to the needs, desires, and dreams of the people they lead. They are energized by the changing environment and create conditions in which people can be their best. Such leaders seek a meaningful future for their people, organizations, and communities. They are flexible, responsive, and able to establish and maintain powerful and positive relationships.

We invite you to chart your own path to resonant leadership and to begin a journey of Intentional Change.[2] As you read this book, you will have the chance to think about where you have been, where you are now, and where you hope to go as you reach for your dreams.

As you embark on this journey, your life will become richer and your leadership more resonant.

Sparking Energy for Change

To begin, think about how you came to be the person you are today, and think about who helped you along the way. "Who Helped Me?" is the first of many exercises in this book. It might be tempting to just *think* about the questions rather than write some notes for yourself. We encourage you to reflect and *write* your thoughts here and throughout the book. While it seems simple, the act of writing is a very important step in this process. Writing causes us to think harder and more deeply, which will provide you with profound insights that will serve you well.

Who Helped Me?

Part 1: Think of the people who have helped you the most in your life and career, the people about whom you would say, "Without this person, I could not have accomplished or achieved as much as I have. Without this person, I would not be the person I am today."

Write their names below. Next to each name, describe moments you remember with them that had a lasting impact on you. What did they say or do? How did you feel at the time? What did you learn from them and from those experiences?

....

....

....

....

....

....

Part 2: Now think of the people who tried to help, manage, or coach you to better performance over the last two years. Think of people who conducted performance reviews with you or gave you feedback on how you were conducting your life or functioning at work.

Write their names and, next to each name, note what the person said or did with you. What did you learn from these people?

....

....

....

....

....

....

Who Helped Me?

Part 3: What feelings did Part 1 of this exercise evoke in you?

....

....

....

....

What feelings or sensations did Part 2 evoke in you?

....

....

....

Compare and contrast the people and situations in Parts 1 and 2. As you consider what each person in these two reflections said or did and how it affected you, what were the differences?

....

....

....

....

What, if anything, do these memories make you want to do today?

....

....

....

....

When people do Part 1 of this exercise, they typically experience warm, emotional reactions to the memories of the individuals who helped them. They remember being deeply affected. They are clear about how these people provoked new dreams and aspirations in them and supported their personal and professional development. Often, individuals remember that the people who helped them did so with compassion, and the feelings stirred by such caring can be deep and intense even years later.

In studying people's reactions to how others have helped them in their lives and at work, we have discovered something interesting about how people change.[3] When we have resonant relationships with our mentors and guides, and when these people act compassionately to support our strengths, positive self-image, and dreams, the impact on us is profound and long-lasting. By helping us connect with our sense of optimism and hope and our personal vision for ourselves—our Ideal Self—we become highly motivated and energized to learn, change, and develop.

But when the act of helping is focused on our weaknesses or deficiencies, we tend to defend ourselves against the person *and* the advice. This often happens in performance conversations, and may be like what you focused on in Part 2 of the exercise. In such situations, we often feel defensive, deflated, or decidedly uninspired. We often ignore the advice and are less likely or, at best, slower to change than when we are focusing on our strengths or our dreams.

The difference in how we react to these two types of help offered to us demonstrates how positive emotions—the Positive Emotional Attractor—are powerful drivers of our energy.[4] Feeling inspired, hopeful, and capable are emotions that enable us to look beyond the problems of today, to creatively seek answers and move to a better future state.

An understanding of how people have helped us learn and grow creates a fascinating set of guidelines for personal and professional development. The contrast between how people acted with you in Part 1 and how they did in Part 2 typically provides insights into how you developed and sustained important changes, and how you might help others do the same. In this book, we will use these insights and our principles of Intentional Change to help you chart a course for meaningful and sustainable leadership development. Following these guidelines and taking the time to do the exercises will help you grow as a person and understand how to support the ongoing development of important people around you.

Leadership Is *Learned*

People often ask us whether leadership can be learned. It is the old nature-versus-nurture question: are people born to be good leaders, or do they develop leadership abilities over time? The answer is yes to both. Some characteristics of good leadership—the tendency to be optimistic, for example—are traits we are probably born with.[5]

But inborn characteristics are few, and even most of these can be enhanced and leveraged (or conversely, underutilized). Far more elements of effective leadership are learned. Of course, family experiences in early childhood, school, community, and work all shape our abilities to build and sustain relationships, guide and manage ourselves, and influence others. We learn critical leadership competencies throughout life. But these abilities never become set in stone: they can and do change, and by intentionally attending to our own development, we do become better leaders.

How and when do people change? People learn and develop when *what they want to change matters deeply and will affect them both personally and professionally.*

In other words, people can become better leaders and can change long-held patterns of behavior. But we have to want to change, and the path we chart for ourselves has to be *personally* meaningful. It's not just about leadership development. In fact, significant professional growth without personal transformation is impossible.

Changing oneself isn't necessarily easy, and it doesn't usually happen quickly. This is because leadership abilities are tied to patterns of behavior related to self-image, relationship skills, and even worldview. These patterns are deep-seated; often we have behaved the same way for so long we are no longer fully aware of what we do or why we do it. But when we have a picture of a future we really want, we discover a path for change and the energy and enthusiasm necessary to sustain the process of reinventing ourselves. This is why creating a clear and compelling life vision is the first and most important step in becoming a resonant leader.

Intentional Change

Significant and sustainable change occurs only when people engage in a *process* of Intentional Change. The process is really a series of discoveries about oneself: one's hopes, dreams, current situation, plans, and supportive relationships to help along the way.

INTENTIONAL CHANGE

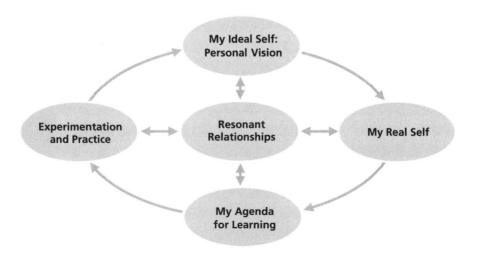

It goes like this: when we (or our organizations, for that matter) really want to change and develop, we need to *first realize or reconnect with what is most important to us and who we are.* This gives us the energy and the motivation to look closely at what is currently working for us and what is getting in our way.

To spark the desire and energy for change, we need to imagine and articulate an *Ideal Self*: who could I be if I were at my very best, living and working effectively, fully, and happily? A meaningful vision of ourselves and our future engages our desire to move toward that future and gives us the courage to try. As you read, reflect on, and do the exercises in this book, the positive feelings you experience when you consider an image of a meaningful, viable future will help power and sustain your drive for growth and change. And, notably, your hunger to achieve your desired future helps you stay engaged, resilient, and flexible in the face of setbacks or other disappointments.

Next, after we have discovered our Ideal Self and Personal Vision, we need to have a clear sense of our *Real Self*: who we are today, our strengths and weaknesses, and how we influence others. Assessing our real selves can be done in many ways, but it requires that we reflect deeply and honestly and engage with others to share perceptions and to receive feedback.

After we have made the first two discoveries, the third discovery is the creation of a plan to address gaps between the real and the ideal and to build on our current strengths. Often we need to learn new skills or expose ourselves to different situations in order to achieve our dreams. Getting from the real to the ideal requires a plan. Our research indicates that people plan in different ways, so these plans must reflect not only how people think about the future, but also how they tend to act when moving toward it.[6] It must be a learning agenda filled with excitement and the joy of discovery, not one with the feeling of obligation of a to-do list.

Then, of course, we need to experiment and practice. Long-lasting behavioral change happens only when people have opportunities to try new behaviors and develop new habits in relatively safe and nonjudgmental environments. This means that we need other people—people who care about us, are interested in our development, and will tell us the truth. We learn best in the context of supportive relationships, so for a change process to work, we need to deliberately include people who can help us maintain focus on our learning agenda.[7]

The Time Is Now

Leaders like you are in positions to make big gains and big mistakes. You have an impact on many people—in your teams, institutions, and communities. You can make a difference when you choose to reach for your personal best, to inspire and energize people, to call them to action, and to reach for a brighter future.

None of this happens by accident. Change—real and sustained change—happens when we have the courage to reach for our dreams and recognize that we might not achieve those dreams unless we, ourselves, change how we are going about leadership *and* life.

Let us begin the journey.

Chapter 2

RESONANT LEADERSHIP

What It Takes

MOST PEOPLE UNDERSTAND *what a leader is supposed to do.* They know what the job entails: scan the environment; build a strategy; organize, execute, and manage resources to get the job done.[1]

Far fewer people understand *how to lead:* how to mobilize energy in people, teams, and other groups; how to inspire and motivate through hope, vision, meaning, and purpose; how to increase productivity while also releasing people's talent, creativity, and resilience; how to build a resonant culture that calls for everyone's best.

Dan Sontag, Senior Vice President at Merrill Lynch, knows how to lead.[2] He is part of a winning team. Wall Street attributes Merrill's private client business success to strategy and execution—the *what* of leadership. Clearly, a brilliant strategy and commitment to goals have been key to victory in the market. Beyond that, though, something else has been happening in the private client business. *How* Dan has led his people to implement the strategy has been marked by creativity, courage, and passion. As head of the Americas Client Relationship Group, he has brought his leadership team to the point that it leverages its strengths and builds resonance even when dealing with organizational challenges.

The earliest years of the twenty-first century were difficult for some financial service businesses. The team at Merrill made some tough choices—tightening controls, changing the teams at the top, and calling for changes in the culture. Dan realized that this last element—culture change—was really going to make the difference and ensure that the success the company had begun to realize could be sustained.

And if culture is to change, the first thing that must be addressed is *how people lead*. Dan took his entire management team through a process of discovering what they needed to do to become resonant leaders of a new culture. How did he do this? First, every manager was interviewed, confidentially, about leadership and culture at Merrill. This information was analyzed for themes that captured people's perceptions about leadership strengths, core values, and aspects of culture that were either helping or hurting the company.

The information painted a clear and challenging picture of the organizational landscape. Dan took this picture to the entire team in a series of truth-telling meetings, culminating in a two-day session in which all 150 managers participated. As Dan led people through a series of intense conversations, they became intrigued with the potential. Would Dan actually address some of the more challenging issues and elephants in the room? Would the managers' individual and collective strengths be seen, or was this process just intended to find the warts? Would it result in improving the culture, or would it just be an exercise?

In the end, the exercise lived up to people's expectations—and beyond. Leaders emerged from the interviews and meetings with far more clarity about what they, as a leadership team, valued and wanted to preserve, as well as what they needed to change. They had enjoyed a positive—and different—experience of leadership because of how Dan organized the meeting and how he engaged with the group. Because of the conversations that day, the managers now held a much clearer picture of the challenges of aligning leadership behavior, culture, and strategy. The leaders experienced renewed energy, a shared language, and new commitment to each other. They felt ready to build on their collective strengths and face the very real issues they had brought to light. They ended stronger than when they started.

What Makes a Great Leader?

Why were these events and conversations so powerful? We think it had something to do with Dan himself. Well before any interviews or meetings were planned, he reflected deeply on what he saw in his organization, what he wanted, and what his own contribution to the culture had been and should be. He did not go into this lightly— he knew that if he opened up the conversation, he would have to take it to the end. He took a risk—a risk he carefully considered and realized was necessary if he was to lead his team to tackle some real issues.

Rarely have we seen a person *lead* as Dan did the day his management team came together. He defined resonant leadership. He listened to his people and really heard them. He inspired trust. He was absolutely, totally clear about his own commitment to issues he felt were not only good for business, but also the right thing to do—and he wasn't going to budge, no matter how hard it might be for the organization and the culture to change. Because he had previously reflected on his own values, he was able to respond clearly and empathetically in the moment, even in the face of some opposing views coming from his team. Through this demonstration of commitment to his values, he inspired people with his courage and created hope through his vision of the future.

What can we learn from leaders like Dan? They recognize the power they have in their role as a leader, and they use it wisely. In other words, Dan recognized that being a leader gave him authority, and he consciously used his authority and his role to shake people up and generate energy and excitement around a new future for the team and the organization.

Research in the areas of psychology, neuroscience, management, and organizational behavior has helped us draw several conclusions about what people can do to enhance their capacity for great leadership. First, behaviors like those that Dan exhibited can be cultivated and learned as well. In the next few pages, you will explore what you have learned through your own experience and how your mental models of power and leadership inform your thinking today.

Owning Your Personal Power

One of the first, and best, lessons about leadership comes when we do exactly what Dan did in the example above. First, we realize that we actually have a good deal of power in our leadership roles, and second, we learn how to manage our own and others' responses to our power and authority. A surprising number of people miss this lesson; they fail to realize that embracing their personal power—formal and informal—is a crucial step in leading successfully.

Why do people miss this lesson? Many of us are just humble enough (or just busy enough) to ignore the impact of the powerful positions we hold in life and at work. In many cultures, it is considered arrogant to openly embrace one's power. Social norms can drive us to minimize our very real authority or to deny that our power truly has an effect on people. Even when we embrace leadership positions in our families, communities, and organizations, we often don't recognize our impact. And then, of course, some people take their power and authority too seriously, and too far. In either case, failure to own our power in a balanced way and to recognize the impact we have on people's actions, perceptions, and emotions can cause us to be far less effective leaders.[3]

Are you too humble about your leadership? Many people are. We see ourselves as normal people, not as leaders whom others look to for direction and inspiration. The following exercise will help you recognize how much power you have and what people really want and need from you as a result.

Who Do You Lead?

1. On the chart on the following page, brainstorm and write a list of several groups that you belong to. Break these groups down as much as you can (e.g., don't just write "family," but note the various branches and groups within your family; instead of writing "work," describe your immediate team, the organization around it, and the groups that you touch or have some responsibility for). Also be sure to list groups where your authority is informal, where your title isn't the only source of your power—consider other arenas where you guide, advise, and help people.

2. Next to each group, label or name your role (e.g., "father" or "mother," "oldest cousin," "team leader," "adviser to the Board," etc.).

3. For each position, formal and informal, describe your role (e.g., "I am the person everyone comes to when there is a conflict in the family"; "I am the one who knows the organization's history"; "I am the designated leader of the Division").

4. For each of your roles, write who looks to you for guidance, help, and vision and what they look for from you. Be as specific as you can (e.g., "My children look to me for love, values, sustenance. . . ."; "My team looks to me to understand their needs, provide help, remove obstacles, and share information"; "My boss looks to me to deliver on my promises").

My Groups	My Role	Description of My Role	People and Groups Who Turn to Me for Help, Guidance, or Direction	What People Look for from Me

By "Who Do You Lead?" we mean the people and groups who depend on you. Have you forgotten any? Have you thought about everything people depend on you for? This might be a daunting task. You probably have a lot more power and authority to make a positive difference than you realize. And if you are like most people, you probably underestimate your impact. Most of us simply do not recognize how many roles we hold or how many people depend on us for leadership or how they are responding to our power.

People who recognize their power tend to use it more consciously and conscientiously. They also tend to have an easier time improving their leadership. So, an important step toward becoming a resonant leader is to embrace your power, examine your assumptions about good leadership, and make some choices about *how* you lead.

Start with Your Beliefs

Ideal
Self

Sacrifice
& Renewal

Real
Self

Mindfulness

Learning
Plan

What Do You Know About Great Leadership?

Chances are you know a lot about leadership—and most of it didn't
come from lessons, school, or management seminars. From childhood on, we attend
carefully to society's heroes and to the people in our lives who have power over us and
who influence us. Over the years, we build a picture in our minds about how leaders
should behave, what they should believe, what they are supposed to do, and even
what they look like. Unconsciously, we develop an approach to leading others that is
based on our mental models of power and leadership. Let's look at your assumptions
and examine your mental models: what do you know about great leaders?

Part 1: Inspirational Leaders

Imagine that you have the ability to travel through time and space and have a conversation with two leaders, past or present, whom you most admire. Who are they? Write
their names. Under each name, write a question you would like to ask him or her. Then,
write the answers you would expect from each of these people. Next, write what each
would say if you asked, "What makes you a great leader?"

Start with Your Beliefs

Part 2: The Best Leaders in My Life

Think about the people with whom, or for whom, you have worked and whom you consider to be great leaders. Write the names of several people who have brought out the best in you. Next to each name, list the qualities, characteristics, and attitudes that you believe make these people great leaders. Be sure to list qualities related to the whole person: mind, body, heart, and spirit. What similarities do you notice among these people?

Start with Your Beliefs

Part 3: Interpreting Your Personal Model of Leadership

If we were to zoom in and analyze your descriptions of the good leaders you have known, it would be clear that you know a lot about leadership. Your knowledge about what works amounts to common wisdom—wisdom you have learned. And a surprising amount of what you know about great leadership is supported by research. In fact, let's take this exercise one step further. Review the list of qualities that you have seen in the best leaders you know. **Organize them on the chart below.**

Self-Awareness: Understands one's own emotions and acts with authenticity and conviction	**Social Awareness:** Understands people, groups, and organizational cultures and is prepared to act on one's understanding of others' needs and desires
Self-Management: Manages positive and negative emotions and achievement orientation and acts with mental clarity and concentrated energy	**Relationship Management:** Guides the emotional tone of a group, builds common bonds, seeks to coach and develop others, and manages conflict

Intellect and Technical Experience: IQ, professional experience, education, and specific skillls related to the job

It is likely that the leadership competencies and qualities you have seen and emulated fit quite comfortably in this "Start with Your Beliefs" chart. What's more, the most important qualities, the ones that really made a difference, are in the top two rows. That is because much of what it takes to excel at leadership has to do with how you manage yourself, build relationships, and bring people together around an optimistic vision of the future.

Resonant leadership is common sense. Why, then, are there so few truly great resonant leaders in our companies and communities? Think of your own experience: How many good managers, bosses, or leaders have you experienced? How many bad? What's the ratio of good to bad? What impact have these people had on you and others?

The Best and Worst Leaders

On the left side of the chart below, list the leaders, bosses, or managers who brought out the best in you. Then, in the "Worst Leaders" column, list a few people whom you have known or worked for and who epitomize bad leadership—people who caused you and others to shut down, underperform, or even fail. Write some notes about how each person typically acted and his or her impact on you and others.

Best Leaders	Worst Leaders

The Best and Worst Leaders

1. Write some notes about what these people (good and bad) typically said or did. How did they make you and others feel?

....

....

....

....

....

2. Now write a few words about how each of these people affected you. What was the impact, and what were the long- and short-term consequences for you? Write a few notes about how you believe these people affected their teams, organizations, or communities.

....

....

....

....

....

3. What conclusions can you draw from your notes? What do you think was motivating the people in your "Best Leaders" category? Your "Worst Leaders" category? Try to get beyond the feelings they engendered in you. What connections can you make between leadership behavior and performance?

....

....

....

....

....

The Truth About Resonant Leadership

You may be asking yourself, "Why were so many of my bosses so bad?" Most of these poor leaders are not evil or cruel. Most are not stupid—quite the contrary. In fact, our experience with leaders has supported an optimistic view of leadership: most people intend to lead responsibly in the service of the common good. Very few people get up in the morning intending to do harm to the people who depend on them.

Why, then, do so many good people fall short of their potential? It might have something to do with people's beliefs about what leaders should be and should do. Sadly, a few myths about leadership are widely held to be true. These myths drive leaders to adopt practices that ruin cultures and discourage people to the point that it is unlikely—even impossible—for people to sustain performance over time. As we look at each myth a bit more deeply in the next section, consider what effect these myths and the truths about good leadership have on you.

COMMON MYTHS AND THE TRUTH ABOUT LEADERSHIP

Myth One	**The Truth**
Smart is good enough	*Intellect and technical knowledge are baseline and do not differentiate great leaders. Emotional and social intelligence make the difference.*

Myth Two	**The Truth**
Your mood does not matter	*Emotions are contagious, and a leader can create resonance and a climate that supports success or can spread emotions that create a dissonant, unproductive, and unhealthy climate.*

Myth Three	**The Truth**
Great leaders thrive on constant pressure	*Sacrifice and power stress are inherent in the leader's role. The best leaders manage the pressure through adopting practices of renewal.*

Myth 1: Smart Is Good Enough

Obviously, you have to be talented, smart, and experienced to lead a complex organization or social system. How could you hope to succeed if you don't understand stakeholders, the environment, your technology, or your numbers? But this is not enough. The research tells us that cognitive intelligence—IQ—is simply baseline. In other words, you have to be smart to get in the door. Competencies related to *emotional and social intelligence*—not IQ, college degrees, or technical experience—are the single most important factors in distinguishing great leadership from average leadership.[4]

Emotional intelligence enables leaders to deal with their own internal responses, moods, and states of mind. Social intelligence informs how we understand and interact with others. Leaders who have developed emotional and social intelligence are effective because they act in ways that leave the people around them feeling

EMOTIONAL AND SOCIAL INTELLIGENCE COMPETENCIES

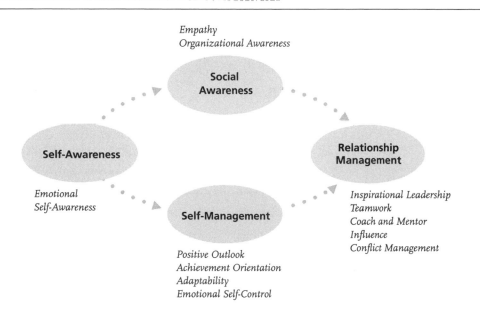

stronger and more capable. These leaders manage themselves effectively under stress and ambiguous circumstances. Intensely in touch with what their people are thinking and feeling, emotionally intelligent leaders motivate and inspire through sharing hope and an optimistic view of the future. At best, they create an environment that is exciting, challenging, and supportive—one that can sustain collective success over the long term.

Self-Awareness: The Foundation of Emotional Intelligence

What do Siddhartha, Socrates, Mohammed, Lao-Tzu, and Goethe have in common? Along with being great philosophers, they all called on us to seek to understand ourselves. But why is it so important to "Know Thyself?"[5] And what does it really mean, anyway?

Emotional self-awareness is the ability to process emotional information quickly and accurately, to recognize one's own emotions as they happen, and to immediately understand their effects on oneself and on others. Good leaders know their strengths, limitations, values, and principles. They believe in their own capability and convey self-assurance and efficacy. Emotional self-awareness is the foundation of emotional intelligence.

And self-awareness provides a solid foundation for self-confidence. Resonant leaders have *presence*: a person notices and trusts them because it is obvious that they know who they are and what is most important to them.[6] They live up to their own standards, a quality that shows in every interaction and decision. This is extremely reassuring to the people they interact with and especially important in times of change or other stress and when there is a need for creative and innovative solutions.

The first step in using emotions to guide our own and others' behavior is to discern our own feelings and moods and their impact on us. This may not be as easy as it seems. Emotions surge through us like electricity, and our brains process information at a rate hard to imagine.

We respond at light speed emotionally, and far more slowly cognitively. In other words, we actually feel before we think. How do *you* know that you are feeling an emotion? Where in your body do you notice it? Which emotions are easy for you to notice, and which are harder for you to discern or describe? Try the "Name Those Feelings" exercise to see how quickly you notice your feelings and how adept you are at articulating your emotions as they happen to you.

Name Those Feelings

1. Imagine you are at work. Think about something that happened recently that caused you to feel strong emotions. Bring the entire situation to mind vividly, including who was there and specifically what was said and done. Bring yourself back to that moment, to the point that you are actually feeling the emotions you felt at the time.

2. What words describe your feelings? Do not analyze or interpret, just name them. At first, you might notice that the words you choose to name your feelings are simple, not nuanced. For example, you may describe your feelings with words like "Stressed," or "Pressured," or "Happy." Push yourself to choose words that describe your feeling exactly, rather than generally. For example, "Stressed" becomes "Frustrated and a little bit anxious," "Happy" becomes "Happy and proud of myself" or "Grateful to my team."

Name Those Feelings

3. What part(s) of your body responds to these emotions? (Note: if you are not sure, check some common "hot spots": stomach, chest, throat, skin temperature/flush, facial muscles.)

4. Now, consider why you felt the way you did in this situation. Go beyond the obvious reasons and generate two or three deeper explanations (e.g., instead of "My boss and I don't get along," it might be, "My boss disrespects me and my people. He has no idea that this project represents years of blood, sweat, and tears," or, "She betrayed my trust").

In today's fast-paced, information-rich world, our capacity to attend effectively to all the information available to us is critical. Our ability to react quickly and accurately to what our bodies and emotions are telling us will separate us from the pack and make us outstanding leaders.[7]

Emotional awareness is important, because at their most basic level, emotions are information. Emotions are the brain's way of making us pay attention to something that appears to be a threat, is attractive to us, or will help us meet a need. From childhood on, we have learned which emotions to attend to and which to ignore. We have also learned how to respond, and most of us have long-standing behavioral responses to certain emotions. These habits serve us well, until they don't. Over time and as our lives and responsibilities change, these patterns may not be as effective as they once were.[8]

Whether you learned about emotions and how to handle them in childhood or later on, that isn't the end of the story. People can, and do, improve their capacity to notice and interpret their own emotions. Improving one's self-awareness will not happen by accident, however. This kind of learning requires adopting a commitment to mindfulness: becoming consciously attuned to oneself, others, and the environment.[9] Mindfulness usually entails adopting regular reflective practices. There are many ways to practice mindfulness, including physical exercise (by oneself), being in nature, prayer, and meditation.

But Self-Awareness Is Not Enough

Recognizing emotion is a good first step in developing emotional and social intelligence.[10] But awareness is never enough. Once we know what we feel, we need to be able to manage our responses. This is more difficult than one might think. Our emotions are powerful drivers of our behavior, and our brains are wired to help us respond quickly to strong emotional signals. This is a simple survival mechanism. In more primitive days, we relied on emotions to tell us to approach other people for contact, love, and caretaking or to flee from danger, freeze, and hide.

Our bodies tend to react just as strongly to real physical dangers as they do to imagined or perceived dangers. Even at work, many people unconsciously respond to organizational and psychological challenges as if their very lives depended on it. This is why even top executives continue to struggle with impulse control. Mastering the ability to accurately scan our environment and respond appropriately is central to effective personal and professional success in to-day's complex and stressful environment.

Unfortunately, it seems that many people do not learn this lesson. Studies have shown that lack of emotional self-control is a major impediment to executive success in organizations.[11] People who become extremely angry do not make good leaders; neither do people who freeze under pressure. People whose emotions seem out of control or inappropriate to the situation do not draw other people to them—they push people away. And people who do not take initiative, maintain focus on a goal, or act consistently from one situation to the next are often perceived as untrustworthy. These people do not create resonance.

As a resonant leader, you need to pay particular attention to your own emotional state and how you affect people. Your power over people is important, and they know it. They are watching you all the time, judging your feelings and moods, and trying to predict what you need, want, and will do. This leads us to the next most common myth—the belief that feelings don't belong at work and that the leader's emotions are not terribly important in determining organizational culture and performance.

Myth 2: Your Mood Does Not Matter

Intelligently using emotion to consistently build relationships and achieve group goals is far more difficult than, say, learning how to read a balance sheet or do financial forecasting. But lots of us have been programmed to believe that we really can eliminate emotion— the soft stuff—from our work lives. We hear this myth all the time, most recently from a well-respected journalist. As he interviewed one of us, he suggested that emotions should never affect leadership: "I understand why a leader needs to have values and understand people. But why should he pay attention to feelings? Isn't it true in business as it is in law that emotions interfere with people's ability to make decisions?"

After we got over our surprise that this well-known reporter actually believed that emotions play no part in work, leadership, or the law, we answered him. Emotions are a natural and constant part of the human experience. We are fooling ourselves if we think we can ignore them. They are everywhere, all the time, driving people to think and act. A leader ignores emotion at his or her peril.

Emotions are contagious. Just as they travel like electricity in our brains and bodies, feelings travel rapidly *between* people. Unlike the closed loop of, say, our circulatory system, emotions are an open-loop system. In other words, your circulatory system has no impact on the circulation of someone standing nearby. Emotions are different. Your emotional state can affect the emotional state of someone standing next to you. We are constantly tuning in to the people and to the general mood around us, and it affects how we feel, what we think, and what we do.[12]

And research suggests that the leader's mood matters most of all.[13] Depending on the leader's span of influence, large groups of people, possibly the entire organization, may carefully emulate the leader's thoughts, beliefs, emotions, and overall mood.

Mood matters. When people are fearful, anxious, or angry, they shut down. When they are generally optimistic, energized, and excited, they think more clearly and creatively, have more resilience, and simply perform better.[14] People's emotions, and the resulting level of resonance, have a profound effect on individual and collective performance, as we can see in how Fred Hassan, CEO of Schering-Plough, leads his people and his company.[15]

One Man's Rules for Resonance

Fred Hassan is a picture of resonant leadership. He is a turnaround artist, one of the few leaders in the world who can take organizations from the brink of disaster to growth, profitability, and organizational health. From Sandoz (Pakistan) Limited to Pharmacia to Schering-Plough, every organization he touches has been left healthier than when he found it.

But how has Fred done it? That phrase—turnaround artist—might evoke an image of a ruthless, in-it-for-the-cash Wall Street type. We've seen a lot of these mercenaries over the years. We have also seen that while they might turn an organization around in the short term, they leave organizations—and the people within—burnt out, burnt up, and unable to sustain success in the long term.

Fred Hassan couldn't be farther away from that dangerous type. The quintessential long-term builder, Fred is highly skilled in the art of building effective relationships. He is principled, oriented to long-term success, curious, courageous, and completely committed to the people in his company. As he puts it, "In my value system, the human factor is most important." He creates an intense social bond among the people who work for him. But he doesn't let anyone become tribal: when you are on Fred's team, he holds you accountable for working for the good of the whole, not just for your part of the organization.

And this tight bond stretches beyond his team, beyond even the top leadership of the company. When he took over at Schering-Plough, the company was failing financially and was being scrutinized by shareholders, analysts, and even the U.S. government. Morale was at an all-time low. After some tough calls and a lot of hard work, the company began to soar: financial results improved exponentially, the business was poised for long-term growth, and the mood of the company had changed completely.

Having surveyed employees annually for their perspectives on critical organizational elements, the company could measure the change in how people felt about management, their jobs, and the company. The survey results were, in fact, surprising and very positive. By 2006, not only had the company sustained double-digit growth for several consecutive quarters, but it had also outperformed all its competitors on critical organizational climate dimensions. In virtually all categories, scores on vital aspects of climate and morale were higher by an unprecedented magnitude.[16] As any leader who has taken a company through the "survival phase" knows, it is highly unusual to come through with people survey results like this.

While Fred would readily admit there isn't a single formula for creating resonance while rebuilding a company, he is also clear about his nonnegotiable rules that have helped him achieve success. These rules guide his decisions and his actions, and they make a difference. What are Fred's rules for resonance?

Don't Accept Life's Scripts

Maybe Fred learned this from his mother, who was one of the first people in their native Pakistan to fight for women's rights and education. Or maybe Fred learned this lesson when he left Pakistan to study in England. Surely the prejudice and stereotypes he encountered there, and later in the United States, might have led him to accept a certain place in society. Not Fred. He proceeded with the confidence that comes from being strong on the inside. He watched, listened, and learned how to manage in multiple cultures. He learned to avoid being pigeonholed. More importantly, he learned never to do this to anyone else. Whether he is in Lincoln, Nebraska, inside the esteemed halls of Harvard, or with a team in Latin America, he looks beyond the stereotypes and trappings and sees people for who they are.

Today, this lesson extends to how he manages his relationships inside his company and in life. He doesn't accept that hierarchy should engender arrogance or drive distance between people. He expects people to build bonds across organizational boundaries. He expects people to treat each other with respect, no matter what their role or function is. He calls on his leaders to employ empathy and emotional intelligence in all their interactions. In fact, with Ron Cheeley, his Senior Vice President of Global Human Resources, Fred has built emotional intelligence into Schering-Plough's performance management systems—you can't succeed at Schering-Plough by being a "typical" manager. You've got to develop emotional intelligence in yourself and others.

Fred holds people accountable for changing the way they approach their own leadership challenges. And he wants people to obtain good outcomes through behaviors that make a person proud. This is related to another of Fred's nonnegotiables: remain open to change, but stick to your principles.

Stay Open, but Let Values Drive All Your Choices

For Fred, this principle-driven openness means that every decision needs to be taken against the backdrop of principles—and these principles need to support organizational health and drive convergence and commitment in people. From his childhood days to the inner circle of corporate America, Fred has faced the world with open eyes—he's studied life's lessons with the goal of learning about himself and about other people. He knows what is most important to him, and these values have driven the major decisions in his life and in business.

When faced with tough times and hard decisions, as he was when he discovered just how broken Schering-Plough was a few years ago, he could always explain his decisions to himself and to others. His decisions were clearly guided by values and good business sense. The result? People trust him quickly, giving him latitude to make dramatic changes. Because he is consistent and holds people at the center of his value system, they feel honored and open to his decisions, and trusting of him. Fred explains this humbly, "I have a way of convincing people to give me a chance, to get on the team. Later, when I have their trust, I can be more assertive. Then, I can ask people to commit for good—'Are you on or off the team?'"

It's Not About Being Nice

Another key to Fred's success is this: he knows that understanding and managing emotion is not the "soft stuff" of leadership. Being highly attuned to emotions and able to use them well does not always mean being "nice." Resonant leaders get sustainable results through *managing emotions, energy, and relationships,* not just from being nice. Leaders like Fred Hassan use the whole spectrum of emotions to challenge people, generate excitement, and hold people accountable. These leaders are not always nice, but they always create an environment in which people are optimistic about the future and will stretch to get there. For Fred, this means a low tolerance for passive resistance, cynical attitudes, or a rock-star mentality. When he encounters these behaviors and sees people's ambition on their sleeves, he will give people clear feedback and a chance to change. If they don't, they find themselves doing something else.

Approach New Challenges with a Positive Attitude

For Fred, work is a passion. He believes that work should never feel as if you are doing a favor for someone else. And he holds this simple truth: when people are having fun at work, they are more successful. Fred's passion is contagious. When you are with him or even read the messages he writes for employees, you can feel his care and concern. His excitement and optimism are tangible. Fred Hassan uses emotion to create a resonant environment that supports healthy interaction, creativity, and productivity. This leads to individual and collective success.

You, like Fred, may have "rules for resonance," or you might be creating them as you read this book. What's most important is that resonant leadership does not happen by accident. That is why it is crucial to understand the next—and maybe the most dangerous—myth about leadership. Too many of us believe that once we have developed the capacity for emotional intelligence and resonant leadership, we are prepared to face anything life throws at us.

Myth Three: Great Leaders Can Thrive on Constant Pressure

We have noticed a growing problem: even good leaders are having a hard time sustaining effectiveness over long periods in the face of the immense challenges they face every day. Too many leaders are slipping into destructive patterns and taking their people with them.

Just a glance at the news reminds us that the world is becoming more unpredictable and unstable. Extreme social pressures, massive industry changes, complex organizational structures, increased pressure from multiple stakeholders—the list goes on and on. At the most personal level, leaders are never unplugged from the demands of work. We have round-the-clock access to e-mail and are never far from our clients' or customers' demands, not to mention our employees' needs. A leader's emotional resources are tapped constantly, and he or she must give unceasingly.

The unending, heavy responsibilities and constant demands can cause a particular kind of stress—*power stress*—which, over time, wears people down. It is inherent in a leadership role and can cause leaders to fall into the *Sacrifice Syndrome*—a vicious cycle of stress and sacrifice, resulting in mental and physical distress, burnout, and diminished effectiveness. And, because emotions are contagious and people take their cues from leaders, it is all too likely that such personal dissonance can easily spread to a team or even the organization. So with the best of intentions, we drive ourselves and our teams toward deadlines, important meetings, the next business trip, not noticing that we're becoming less optimistic, less hopeful, and more exclusively task focused. We take relationships for granted, and before we know it, we have lost our edge and our capacity for resonant leadership. We are no longer as effective as we could be.

So how can we avoid power stress and the Sacrifice Syndrome? The answer lies in how we manage our roles and the accompanying stress and sacrifice. To cope effectively, leaders need to cultivate habits of the mind and behavior that counter the negative effects of stress and constant sacrifice. In other words, to sustain resonant leadership, we must understand the vital role that *renewal* plays in sustaining effectiveness.

Several practices help us stop the Sacrifice Syndrome before it stops us. These practices start with mindfulness, hope, and compassion. *Mindfulness* means learning to live in a state of reflection and

POWER STRESS

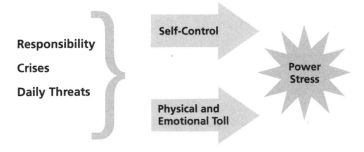

Dissonance can become the default

openness, in which we are tuned in to self, others, and our environment. This does not mean just resting or taking holidays. Rather, mindful practices enable true renewal, which is about reconnecting to aspects of ourselves and the rest of the world that inspire us and bring out our best qualities. It is about allowing ourselves time to attend to our needs. This requires conscious attention and action, and more than simple maintenance.

The process of renewal begins with mindfulness, but there is more. Research shows that consciously engaging certain experiences and emotions, such as hope and compassion, counters the physiological and psychological harm done by stress. These experiences increase our resilience, physically and psychologically, even in the face of challenges.[17]

Hope is what we experience when we look forward to a future that seems feasible and enticing. Think back to a time when you were beginning a new and exciting phase of life—that first good job, when you first fell in love, the birth of your first child. You no doubt felt hopeful as you anticipated the future, even if you also felt a bit of

SUSTAINING RESONANCE AND EFFECTIVENESS THROUGH THE SACRIFICE-RENEWAL CYCLE

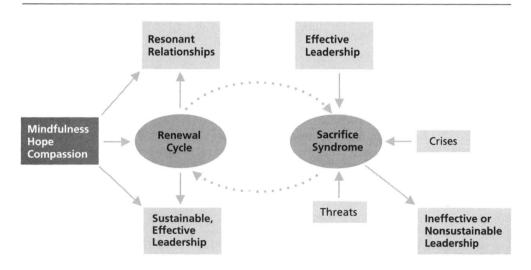

concern about how life would change and whether you were up to the task. Hope carries us through transitions in life. It gives us energy and resilience and helps us face the future with courage.

People who have a positive vision of where they are going are more likely to have a sense of purpose. Because of this sense, they can work toward their goals, even when things are difficult. This is true for groups as well. A team with a positive and hopeful view of where it needs to go, a clear sense of purpose and direction, and resonant relationships can achieve great things while bringing out the best in each person.

And then there is *compassion*—not often discussed in books on leadership. But compassion is a very important aspect of the human experience and human relationships. Compassion is empathy in action. Like hope, it sparks positive physiological changes that counter the negative effects of stress. Like hope, compassion triggers renewal for the individual and is contagious. Both hope and compassion create personal resonance. They also influence group and organization climate, inspiring others to reach for collective goals and support one another along the way.

People who can sustain effectiveness over time understand that they are not superheroes and that they must attend to renewal as a normal and natural part of life. So, as you consider developing your capacity for great leadership, it will serve you well to examine how you renew yourself, as well as how you use your emotional intelligence and the power of emotion to guide your behavior and the behavior of others.

Resonance or Dissonance: The Leader's Choice

Resonance is a powerful collective energy that reverberates among people and supports higher productivity, creativity, a sense of unity, a sense of purpose, and better results.[18] The opposite of resonance is dissonance. Dissonant environments are marked by negative emotions like fear, anger, anxiety, pessimism, and often extreme individualism.

Whether they know it or not, leaders who create dissonant environments frequently drive people toward antagonism, hostility, and alienation. These leaders create a toxic work environment in which people feel self-protective and consequently perform poorly. Dissonant leaders are often commanding and use top-down or micromanaging approaches. They focus relentlessly on details and immediate results, to the exclusion of nearly everything else. And, even though these leaders may be effective in the short run, in the long run they wreak havoc on the emotional climate, strangle individual potential, and drive overall results down.

Some leaders create dissonance in a much less obvious way. Rather than ranting or micromanaging, they seem on the surface to be open, supportive, and even democratic in their approach. In actuality (and often as a result of wanting to be liked by everyone), they are far too vague, indecisive, or inconsistent and scattered. These leaders may seem friendly and approachable, but they just don't get anything done. They leave people feeling frustrated, confused, and even scared—no one knows what he or she is supposed to be doing or who is in control. In these situations, people's natural desire to contribute, achieve, and grow is thwarted by poor leadership. As a result morale and productivity suffers.

Organizations whose cultures and leaders support resonance drive groups toward optimism, are attuned to people's feelings, and move those feelings in a positive direction. Such leaders—like Fred Hassan—speak authentically from their own values and resonate with the emotions of those around them. Resonant leaders negotiate the challenges of constant change and leave people feeling uplifted, even in difficult times. Through resonant leadership, vision and hope are brought to the organization as the leaders pay attention to providing what is needed at the time, whether it is more structure, decisiveness, clarity, encouragement, open dialogue, or transparency. Resonant leaders manage negative emotions, using them carefully, consciously, and appropriately. As importantly, the leaders use their positive emotions to renew themselves and to create positive relationships and a healthy, vibrant environment. Because they expect and get results, resonant leaders leave their people and organizations stronger and readier to face the future.

As you read this chapter, you may have been considering the degree to which *you* create resonance and how you do it. Take some time now to answer the questions in the last exercise of this chapter.

Am I a Resonant Leader?

If you are wondering if you are a resonant leader, ask yourself these questions:

Am I inspirational? How do I inspire people?

....

....

....

Do I create an overall positive emotional tone that is characterized by hope? How?

....

....

....

Am I in touch with others? Do I really know what is in others' hearts and on their minds? How do I show this?

....

....

....

Do I regularly experience and demonstrate compassion? How?

....

....

....

Am I authentic and in tune with myself, others, and the environment? How can people see this in me?

....

....

....

Resonant leadership is common sense, but it is not common practice. This is probably because most of us operate on false assumptions about what it takes to be a great leader—including the myths that good leaders should be able to take the heat, that emotions don't matter, and that intellectual prowess will carry the day.

Leadership is a conscious process, starting with clarity about one's own personal vision and hopes for the future. Resonant leadership requires that a person be highly self-aware, manage himself or herself in stressful and complex environments, read other people, empathize with their needs, and lead others to get the job done. Resonant leaders need to know what inhibits effective individual and team performance and how to address these issues. In other words, leadership requires emotional and social intelligence and a deep understanding of how social systems—and the people in them—must work together to achieve complex and challenging goals.

In the next chapter, you will continue to explore your leadership. You will reflect on how you are currently attending to aspects of who you are, inventory your leadership strengths, listen for wake-up calls, and continue to chart a course toward developing an inspiring vision of the future for your Ideal Self.

Chapter 3

LISTENING TO YOUR WAKE-UP CALLS

Staying Awake, Aware,
and Ready to Learn

Some people don't wait around for life's harsher wake-up calls—the broken relationships, failures, and health problems. Instead, these people stay tuned in by using life's laboratory to keep themselves awake, aware, and learning. We call this *mindfulness.*[1] People who deliberately practice mindfulness are consciously self-aware and self-monitoring; they are open and attentive to other people and to the world around them. They tend to be resilient and strong in the face of power stress, because they attend to personal renewal as a way of life. They also learn from experiences faster and better than most people do.

C. J. Warner of BP is just such a person.[2] As Group Vice President, C. J. is one of very few senior women in the oil and gas industry. She is a chemical engineer and a "techie"—a person who identifies strongly with her profession and with the people who work in her industry. An excellent leader, she deftly builds relationships between disparate groups and finds paths through difficult situations. C. J. gets results and builds resonance.

Managing her career in a male-dominated industry has had its challenges. For example, her career has included numerous assignments and responsibilities that were presented as necessary developmental steps to help ensure her success—although clearly all these steps weren't typically present in the career paths of her male counterparts.

C. J. could have allowed these extra hurdles to frustrate her, make her angry and bitter, or cause her to retreat either into herself or away from the industry. But she chose to use her experiences to *learn*. With eyes wide open, she has walked into each new situation with clear intention: Get results. Build relationships. Maintain unflagging commitment to values. She treats challenges as opportunities—weighing what needs to happen to achieve results against how to strengthen her people. Her intention is to leave her team and her organization stronger for the experience and more able to face the next challenge.

C. J. has had many opportunities to learn how to bring people together around the goals she sees as critical. She has successfully built bridges between people and organizations where tough, direct confrontation is the standard practice—as it can be between the oil industry and the various regulatory bodies in the United States. In one high-stakes situation, she personally built relationships on both sides of the fence, arguing for cooperation and collaboration around their larger mutual goal—a cleaner environment. She actively modeled behavior and a stance that was not adversarial, but relational. One by one, she managed to convince stakeholders in the regulatory agency, in her company, and elsewhere that working together would be far better and far more successful than battling over every detail. The outcome: in a relatively short time, the parties worked out an agreement that improved environmental performance and established a pattern eventually followed by the entire U.S. industry. And everyone felt good about it.

What's different about C. J. is that, whether she is facing a challenge or an opportunity, she is constantly tuning in to what is going on for her, with others, and in her environment. C. J. keeps her eyes open. She knows what she needs to do, and she achieves results while learning and helping people feel stronger and more capable for their contact with her. Maybe in part because she faced special challenges as a female engineer, and then a female executive in the oil industry, she adopted a very effective strategy early on. Rather than lashing out or shutting down, she decided to open up to each new experience. She consciously and deliberately takes each opportunity to learn and to grow, every day and with every challenge. This is mindfulness at its best.

Mindfulness:
Awake, Aware, and Attending

Sustaining mindfulness in the midst of constant career and life pressures is not easy. It helps to include a few simple structures in your daily routine. One way to build these structures and practices into life is to think about yourself holistically—to consider how to attend to the body, mind, heart, and spirit. As a way to begin looking at how tuned-in you are to your current situation, complete the following survey and the two exercises that follow. Each of them will cause you to reflect on your life holistically. The "Taking Stock" survey directs your thoughts to what you value in life and work and what may be dragging you down. The "Mindfulness Check-In" exercises take you a bit deeper so that you can think about how consciously you attend to yourself as a whole person.

Taking Stock

Building Mindfulness Through a Personal Inventory

What activities do I consider of greatest worth in my life?

....

....

....

....

....

What activities do I consider of greatest worth in my work?

....

....

....

....

....

What am I currently doing in my life that I like?

....

....

....

....

....

Taking Stock

What am I currently doing in my work that I like?

_____

_____

_____

_____

_____

_____

What am I currently doing in my life that I don't like?

_____

_____

_____

_____

_____

_____

What am I currently doing in my work that I don't like?

_____

_____

_____

_____

_____

_____

_____

Mindfulness Check-In

Mind

Write for two minutes without stopping about your current thoughts.
What comes easily to mind? What do you not want to think about today?

....

....

....

....

....

....

....

....

....

Body

Trace this sketch of the body with your pen or pencil and, as you do,
scan your physical body, noticing areas of tension, relaxation, sore-
ness, or good feelings. Circle areas that need your attention.

....

....

....

....

....

Mindfulness Check-In

Heart/Emotions

Write a list of your current feelings. Where do you feel emotions in your body? What do you need to continue doing today to feel emotions that serve you and are useful? What do you need to attend to in order to minimize or change your feelings if they are distressful and are not serving you?

....

....

....

....

....

....

....

Spirit

Close your eyes and picture something or someone who inspires you. Sit with this feeling as you take a few very deep breaths. What images came to your mind? How do these images inspire you to act today? Imagine yourself radiating this image today. What will you say, think, and do?

....

....

....

....

....

....

....

....

You have now completed a scan of your holistic self—mind, body, heart, and spirit. The "Seeking Balance" exercise will help you get a sense of how balanced you are and will invite you to take a few minutes to reflect on how satisfied you are with your current state.[3] And if you desire, use the "Mindful Change" exercise to explore ways of achieving the balance and focus you need to be at your best.

Seeking Balance

Attending Mindfully to All Aspects of My Self

The Medicine Wheel is a tradition found in virtually all land-based cultures around the world, although it is depicted in many diverse forms. "Medicine" refers to all that is "good" and life giving. The four quadrants—North (Physical), East (Spiritual), South (Emotional), and West (Mental) represent perfect balance. Spiritual and self-development occur as a result of attending to and challenging oneself in each area.[a]

Use the Medicine Wheel to guide your thinking about the various activities you currently engage in—mind, body, spirit and emotion. Draw pictures or use key words to depict what you are currently doing to feed and express the various aspects of your self and what you would like do more often or more fully.

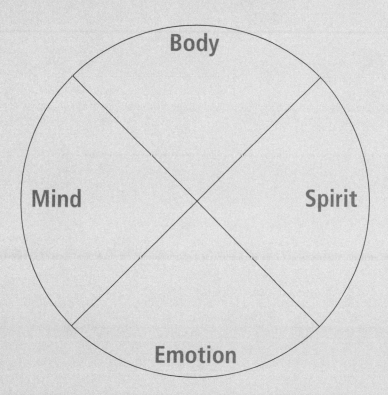

a. See C. Clinton Sidle, The Leadership Wheel: *Five Steps for Achieving Individual and Organizational Greatness* (New York: Palgrave MacMillan, 2005); see also Angeles Arrien, *The Four-Fold Way: Walking the Paths of the Warrior, Teacher, Healer, and Visionary* (New York: HarperCollins, 1993).

Fine-Tuning Beliefs and Behavior

Look at your Medicine Wheel and consider how you attend to your mind, body, spirit, and emotion and how you would like to balance your life. Answer these questions:

What do you want more of in your life and what do you want less of? Do you need to simplify or intensify? If so, in which area of your life? If you really want to chart a path to personal balance, what must you do?

....

....

....

....

What change in limiting beliefs will help you progress toward the achievement of greater balance? Examples of limiting beliefs: "I don't have time to exercise every day," or, "I just can't reconcile with my brother. He won't let me."

....

....

....

....

What must you give up, sacrifice, eliminate, or let go of in order to achieve the balance you want?

....

....

....

....

If you found the last few exercises easy, then chances are you have developed habits that allow you to maintain mindfulness as a normal part of life. But if you are like most people, you may have found that reflecting on yourself holistically is challenging. Over the course of our busy adult lives, many of us lose sight of various aspects of ourselves. Some of us wake up one day and find that we are out of shape and overweight. Or maybe we have lost touch with an artistic or spiritual practice that sustained us for many years. Or maybe we just don't feel as sharp as we once did. How can this happen to smart people? It happens because in the face of our complex lives and leaders' responsibilities, we can slip into the Sacrifice Syndrome without even realizing it.

The Sacrifice Syndrome and the Slippery Slope

Today, Matt Doherty is a successful and well-respected basketball coach at Southern Methodist University.[4] A resonant leader, he is liked and respected by players, fans, and alumni. He's had an interesting career, but for a while, it seemed that things weren't going his way at all.

Matt was named head coach of the University of North Carolina (UNC) men's basketball team in 2000. This position was a dream job—one of the top college basketball teams in the world, a perennial champion with an extremely rich tradition. He was a veteran of the program, having played with Michael Jordon on the 1982 national championship team. Matt was a great player and a great young coach.

As one of UNC's youngest coaches, Matt stood at the helm of a tremendously complicated program—logistically, emotionally, and politically. Though a surprise choice for the position, he impressed the fans, players, and press with his intensity and focus. He was eager to prove himself and not let anyone down. He drove the players hard, and himself harder, relishing the pressure of being responsible for a team that many people felt personally passionate about. Matt worked tirelessly and achieved early success, beating Kansas, a perennial championship team, in front of a rabid crowd at Madison Square Garden. He was in his element.

But there were some bumps in the road, even early on. A few people were grumbling about the changes he had made at the university; others were questioning why, for example, he had brought in his own coaching staff and reorganized the administrative staff. Matt failed to notice or care that not everyone was happy with his decisions—he was on a mission.

Failure was not an option—either in his mind or in the minds of the powerful stakeholders who were part of the UNC basketball extended family—former players and coaches; alumni, students, and other fans; and the current players, many of whom had professional aspirations. Every day, there were practices to plan, high school players to recruit, and college players to deal with. Halfway through his third season, his star player got hurt and the team lost a few close games. The "family" was not used to losing, and neither was Matt.

As the pressure mounted, so did Matt's drive and focus. Soon, his famous intensity became a liability. He had slipped into the Sacrifice Syndrome without even knowing it. He was in a state of constant power stress with all its consequences. As the weeks and months wore on with no letup, he couldn't sleep or exercise or even spend quality time with his family.

Always a strong and emotional person and coach, he slipped into yelling and losing his temper with players, referees, and even opposing coaches. Each episode was rehashed in the press, on Web sites, and on the radio. Nobody was happy, and Matt had lost perspective—literally; he was in a perpetual state of hypervigilance and sensitivity. And the team kept losing.

After the team failed to make the NCAA Tournament, Matt was forced to resign, and his world came crumbling down. For a while, he didn't know if he would ever want to coach again. It was a difficult time and a real wake-up call.

He vowed to at least learn from the experience, turning his signature drive and intensity toward figuring out what had happened. He solicited input from family, friends, and colleagues—even a few who may have helped orchestrate his demise. He took time off. After he found an executive leadership coach, Matt worked hard on the reflective exercises the coach set for him. First in safe environments and then increasingly out in the real world, Matt practiced new behaviors. He dedicated himself to understanding what had happened, who he was, and what he wanted.

Now, Matt is coaching again at a prestigious school, this time with a new set of skills for managing his own emotions and the emotions of others. These resonant leadership practices help him maintain balance in all aspects of life. Specifically, he is living and coaching in a way that is consistent with his values. Though still strong and intense, he now controls his intensity, rather than having it control him. He enjoys basketball again and loves helping to shape and mold young players. At SMU, he has built a successful basketball program that is based on his core values of respect, trust, and commitment. He has become a resonant leader, and his teams are winning.

As Matt's story shows, it is easy to slip into mindlessness, even if we are talented and committed and have the capacity to create resonance. As we attempt to respond to the many demands placed on us in very uncertain environments, our stress mounts past the point that our bodies are equipped to handle it physically, psychologically, or emotionally. Add to this scenario the fact that our tactics for dealing with (or, more accurately, avoiding) this stress simply compound the problem. Soon we find ourselves trapped in the Sacrifice Syndrome. We are overdrawn physically, mentally, emotionally, and often spiritually.

Resonant leaders regularly monitor themselves, to see if they might be slipping toward the Sacrifice Syndrome. By paying attention to this potential pitfall early, we can stop problems before they start. An easy way to monitor yourself is to periodically do the next exercise.

The Sacrifice Syndrome

Sacrifice & Renewal

Ideal Self

Real Self

Mindfulness

Resonant Leadership

Learning Plan

Where Am I?

The Sacrifice Syndrome can be insidious, and it is sometimes hard to tell we are slipping into it until we are caught. If we are vigilant, however, we can see signs that we are heading in the wrong direction before it becomes a problem. Check the following list. Many of these clues can help you determine if you are heading toward the Sacrifice Syndrome, so you can catch yourself before you slide into dissonance.

I am:

☐ Working harder with less result

☐ Getting home later or leaving home earlier each day

☐ Feeling tired, even after sleeping

☐ Having trouble falling asleep, or waking up in the middle of the night

☐ Finding less time (or no time at all) for the things I used to enjoy

☐ Rarely relaxed, and/or only really relaxed with alcohol or drugs

☐ Drinking more coffee

☐ Unable to take my vacation days

I have noticed changes in myself or my relationships, such as:

☐ I can no longer really talk about my problems with my spouse or partner

☐ I don't care what I eat, whether too much or too little

☐ I can't remember the last time I had a long conversation with a trusted friend

☐ My children have stopped asking me to attend their functions or games

☐ I no longer attend my place of worship or find time for quiet contemplation

☐ I don't exercise as much as I used to

☐ I don't smile or laugh as much as I used to

I do:

☐ Have frequent headaches, backaches, or pain

☐ Routinely take over-the-counter antacids or painkillers

☐ Feel as if nothing I do seems to matter anymore or have the impact I want

☐ Feel as if no one can understand what I need to do or how much work I have

☐ Sometimes feel numb or react inappropriately to situations with strong emotions

☐ Feel too overwhelmed to seek new experiences, ideas, or ways of doing things

☐ Frequently think about how to escape my current situation

Coping with Power Stress and the Sacrifice Syndrome

If you are like most people, you have developed ways to cope with the everyday pressures of your job and the longer-term threat posed by power stress and the Sacrifice Syndrome. Many of us rely on personal resilience and the coping mechanisms that we learned and were rewarded for as we grew into adulthood. Some of us rely on personal strengths to carry us through crises, and this often works, for a while. But any strength taken to the extreme can become a weakness. For example, Matt's signature intensity contributed to his inability to modulate his emotions or read the environment. Matt hated losing and intensely wanted to perform well. When the team's fortunes changed, his stress went up disproportionately and he coped by doing more of what he always did—pushing himself and others as hard as possible.

Others among us simply shut down when we feel or think that something is intolerable or scary. Thoughts such as "I need to exercise or I might have a heart attack," or "I need to work less, because my kids are really upset with me," or "This project will be canceled because I can't influence my boss" can increase our anxiety. Usually, we have some intellectual understanding that we need to change something, and we may even have the emotional desire, but somehow we can't open up and deal with what is happening—we are stuck and resistant to change.

It actually makes sense: resistance is about protection. But while resistance can decrease our anxiety momentarily, it can also cause us to act self-destructively. The situation is paradoxical and dangerous.

So, it is important to know how and when our coping mechanisms constitute unhealthy resistance. Most of us have tendencies that drive how we deal with stress and resist anxiety. These tendencies are called defensive routines, which we adopt to help us feel more in control.[5]

While we may vary our response to stress a bit, most of us have habitual coping strategies. These are often affected by our tendency to either internalize or externalize feelings and problems and to either approach or avoid the issues. If you tend to *internalize your feelings and problems* when under pressure, you will often rely even more on yourself than usual and fail to get any outside perspectives on your situation. If you tend to *externalize your feelings and problems*, you may over-rely on others, get distracted easily, or place blame for the problems outside yourself. When there are stressful situations and you tend to *approach problems,* you will rush to solve or respond; if you tend to *avoid problems,* you may wait too long to deal with things or may even ignore issues. The next exercise on defensive routines will help you identify your defensive pattern and gain insight into how you typically respond to stressful feelings or problems.

My Defensive Routines

How I Cope with Pressure and Problems

Step 1: What do you tend to do when under pressure?
Check all that apply to you.

Approach and Internalize
- ☐ I get to work earlier and stay at work later
- ☐ I continue to add new projects or take on more roles despite a realistic shortage of time or results
- ☐ I constantly remind myself of my own or others' high standards for me
- ☐ I expect everyone to perform at my high standards
- ☐ I can never say "no"

My Defensive Routines

Avoid and Internalize

- ☐ I move further inside: my office, my projects, my thoughts and concerns
- ☐ I become detached from relationships with colleagues, friends, and family
- ☐ I communicate less than usual and only about what I feel is essential
- ☐ Only my mission and goals seem important
- ☐ I don't need input from others
- ☐ I feel that other people just get in the way

Approach and Externalize

- ☐ I am the only one who knows the answer
- ☐ If anyone disagrees with me I will disregard them or make them sorry for disagreeing
- ☐ My closest friends and advisers always agree with me
- ☐ I never waver on decisions

Avoid and Externalize

- ☐ I focus on negative aspects of situations
- ☐ I wear anger and disappointment as a badge of honor
- ☐ I criticize or become cynical with those who want things to change or have hope
- ☐ I blame my mood/circumstances on the situation or someone else
- ☐ I enjoy being with like-minded people and talking about what we think is wrong

Step 2: Circle the five check marks that indicate your primary ways of dealing with life and work when you are stressed. These are defensive routines—they help you defend yourself from your stressors and may inhibit change. The next step will help you unravel the impact of these habits.

Step 3: On the following page, list your top five defensive routines and note whether they are linked with approaching or avoiding issues or your feelings, and whether you tend to internalize or externalize your responses. Then, write some notes about how your routines affect you, people close to you, and possibly your organization.

My Defensive Routines	Approach, Avoid, Internalize, Externalize	How this affects me: mind, body, emotion, spirit	How this affects my team/close colleagues, family	How this affects the degree of resonance or dissonance in my environment

A first step in managing your defensive routines is to recognize what they are. In the exercise, you noted some of the ways you habitually respond and how these patterns of behavior affect you and others. The next step is to ask yourself, "Are these habits serving me or others well?" While sometimes our defensive routines are in fact helpful, many times they are not. If you notice that your habits are not helping you or others, you will need to focus on your behavior, monitoring when and how you respond to people and issues. Ideally, you will become more conscious of your choices *before* you act.

Defensive routines and a natural tendency to protect ourselves can be counterproductive. Instead of keeping us safe, these habits can cause us to become mindless and resistant to change. That's where wake-up calls come in: when we attend mindfully to the clues and cues in our environment, we are more likely to manage ourselves in ways that allow us to achieve balance as we face life's challenges.

Wake-Up Calls

Partly because of our busy lives, most of us are not as mindful as we should or could be. This is where wake-up calls can help us. Wake-up calls can be big and negative, like a heart attack, a divorce, or losing a job. They can be big and positive, like getting married, having a child, or being promoted at work. More often, however, life's wake-up calls are small and hard to hear, like noticing that you are not laughing as much as you did in the past.

The challenge is being able to hear and respond to a wake-up call, and not hitting the snooze button on your alarm clock so that you can return to relative mindlessness. The next exercise is a way to double-check whether you have been able to benefit from wake-up calls you may have heard lately.

Sacrifice & Renewal

Ideal Self

Real Self

Mindfulness

Resonant Leadership

Learning Plan

Attending Mindfully to Life's Messages

The objective of this exercise is to help you reflect on possible wake-up calls and to seek to understand what they might mean for you.

In the left-hand column, review aspects of your life and work:

   a) List any signs of discomfort, unease, restlessness, and/or a vague sense that all is not great in your life (this is a much higher standard than merely "all is not well"); and

   b) Allow yourself to reflect and consider all aspects of life.

In the middle column, write some notes: how do you feel about each of these signs or indicators? Be as specific as you can in describing the feeling. Then ask yourself, "Am I sure that is what I feel?" You can then edit what you wrote to make your answer more accurate.

In the right-hand column, consider and write about what it would take to transform your feeling to one of excitement, hope, optimism, joy, or elation about each aspect of your life or work? Be as specific as possible.

List any signs or indicators that your life or work is anything other than great or ideal.	How do you feel about this? Be as specific as you can.	How can you change the feeling to one of hope, excitement, or elation? Describe the change in as much detail as possible.
Career		
Current Job		

Wake-Up Calls

List any signs or indicators that your life or work is anything other than great or ideal.	How do you feel about this? Be as specific as you can.	How can you change the feeling to one of hope, excitement, or elation? Describe the change in as much detail as possible.
Company/Organization		
Physical Health		
Family		
Friends		
Spiritual Well-Being		

Wake-Up Calls

List any signs or indicators that your life or work is anything other than great or ideal.	How do you feel about this? Be as specific as you can.	How can you change the feeling to one of hope, excitement, or elation? Describe the change in as much detail as possible.
Community		
Other		

Wake-up calls are nature's way of alerting us to pay attention to our behavior, attitudes, values, and relationships. As you have discovered in this chapter, these calls can be big, loud, and initially negative, like Matt's losing his job, or a relationship's ending in divorce. They can be big and positive, like the birth of a child, or an event that suddenly makes you profoundly reconsider how you spend your time.

Wake-up calls can also be subtle—shifts in perspective that can result in your losing sight of important values and elements of your holistic self and possibly slipping into the Sacrifice Syndrome. Either way, wake-up calls tell us that something is out of balance and that there might be an opportunity to reassess, renew, and reconnect with core values and vision.

We all have times in our lives when we need a wake-up call, times when our defensive routines and response to stress have narrowed our perspective and sense of possibility. That is because wake-up calls help us remain mindful. And when we are attuned to ourselves and the world around us, we can use life as a learning laboratory—one that supports us in caring for ourselves holistically, integrating the various parts of ourselves in the service of living a full and effective life. By doing so, we increase the likelihood that we can sustain resonance with others.

Through the practices of mindfulness and the process of Intentional Change described here, you can learn to remain open to life's messages. With these actions, you will be more able to consciously step into the future—the future that you desire.

In the next chapter, you will explore that future. You will continue to use reflective exercises to support renewal and mindfulness. And now, you will begin to move from reflection to action and reinvention as you focus on what is most important to you—your values, beliefs, hopes, and dreams.

Chapter 4

SEEING YOUR DREAM

Building an Energizing Personal Vision

JAMES WAS CONFUSED about his future.[1] On the surface, he was doing fine and his path was predictable. Having grown up in a poor neighborhood, he had done much better than most of his friends. He had gone to college, gotten one good job after another, and now, as Vice President of information technology (IT) at a mid-sized company, he was successful and on the high-potential list. James had a loving relationship with his daughters and was prepared to pay for their college tuition. He was divorced, but on amiable terms with his former wife. He had a girlfriend. He was devout in his faith and contributed his time eagerly to church projects. So what was wrong?

The problem was that James no longer found excitement in his work or even in certain other aspects of his life. And when he looked into his future, beyond a few months, it was a blank wall. When we asked him about his hopes and plans, he had a hard time answering the question.

After a long silence, he shrugged his shoulders. This seemed incongruous: a well-dressed, well-respected executive acting like a teenager who does not know what he wants to study in college. So we pushed, "If you won the lottery, say, eighty million dollars, what would you do?" His answer: "I'd drive a truck cross-country." This seemed like an escape fantasy. The sad conclusion was that he wasn't happy and he wanted to escape from work and from the parts of his life that had simply become routine and boring. And yet he wasn't consciously moving toward anything.

But how and why had James lost his passion for work and even for his life? As happens with most people, this change had come about insidiously. He hadn't noticed. We worked with him to look at his current life and where he might like to go. A bit later, he responded to a question about what would make him feel that he was fulfilling his purpose in life, "Teaching high school kids, in the inner city, that computers can be their instruments to freedom."

All of a sudden, his entire demeanor changed. His eyes brightened, he leaned forward, and he started talking faster than we'd heard in months. The excitement was contagious—we could see and feel that James had just had an epiphany. Possibilities opened up. He talked about how he might teach workshops at local high schools in the evening or on weekends. He talked about setting up IT internships for high school students at local companies. It was as if a dam had opened and ideas were pouring in. His image of his career and future changed from "been there, done that," to "Wow, I can't wait to get started." James now had a dream of what he could be and do. He even had some good ideas about how to get there.

There are millions of people like James. They want more from life and work, but are puzzled about how to reach that elusive goal. Or they believe they should be satisfied with the present state of things and don't have the right to ask for more. Others strive for a better future—with the best of intentions, they attend training programs, earn MBAs, and hire coaches to help. In all these situations, though the excitement and intention is real, the efforts tend to be quick fixes that bear little fruit over time. In other words, the degree of lasting change is typically very small.

Parallel situations occur on a personal level. For example, some people go on diets and pay a personal trainer so that they can lose weight or get into better physical condition. At first, they count calories, work out, and weigh themselves regularly. Soon the effort becomes burdensome and feels like constant deprivation, or a regimented schedule at the gym becomes, ultimately, uninspiring and not sustainable. All the good intentions slowly slip away as old eating habits reappear and exercise becomes a chore.

It is easy to get caught up in short-term fixes as we earnestly try to overcome our deficiencies or address our weaknesses. When this happens, we can become trapped by the negative energy generated by overfocusing on our shortcomings or disappointments. Over time, we can become dispirited and, like James, we become restless, stalled, and frustrated with ourselves.

This pattern can spark a self-fulfilling prophesy: when we focus on what is wrong in the present moment, we often lose sight of our dreams and lose our capacity to hope for a better future and to change. Dreams provide energy and direction to guide us to a better life. When we lose sight of an image of our future, we lose our passion and, with it, our energy. The cycle can only spiral downward.

We Become What We Dream

Our dreams help to determine what we become, because a compelling and meaningful vision provides us with the optimism, strength, energy, and efficacy we need to move confidently toward the future. By thinking about what is possible, we experience hope and release a multitude of positive emotions.[2] These positive emotions create energy for our actions and catalyze positive self-perpetuating sequences that feel good and are essential for lasting change.

Engaging the *Positive Emotional Attractor*—including hope—is a complex set of physiological, emotional, cognitive, perceptual, and behavioral responses.[3] This supports a sustainable change process by increasing our capacity for emotional flexibility, improving our neurological functioning, and increasing our sense of psychological well-being. Engaging the Positive Emotional Attractor also counters the effects of power stress, thereby supporting our physical and psychological health.[4]

So, a personal vision *can* spark and help sustain personal change. Indeed, many world-class athletes use visualization techniques and positive thought to bring about their victories and reach their best personal performance.[5] We can apply visualization to cultivate hope in our lives and to begin to realize our dreams.[6] A personal vision triggers a sense of emotional renewal and helps guide our decisions and actions. The key is that the vision should evoke in our mind a specific, clear picture of the future—one that we find inspiring and feasible. A sense of purpose or meaning in our life and work often naturally follows from such images.

A personal vision is the deepest expression of what we want in life. It is a description of our preferred future. In this sense, our personal vision should describe not only what we want out of life and work, but also what kind of person we want to be. Instead of a forecast of what we think is likely in the future, our personal vision is a description of the future we dream about.

Our personal vision is born of becoming clear about our Ideal Self: our noble purpose in life, our dreams and images of a desired future, our passion, and our calling. This ideal is supported by aspects of our core identity and our life and career stage—these define who we are. It is also supported by our belief that we can actually have an impact on our lives and the world around us. The combination of self-efficacy and an optimistic vision of a feasible future sparks hope.[7]

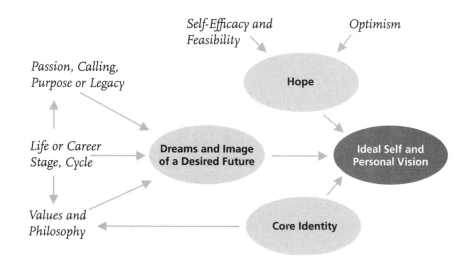

Having a personally inspiring vision helps you see how you can make a positive contribution to the world. What makes the world a better place for your being with us? The answer to this question is probably linked to your sense of calling, mission, or purpose in life. As a way to craft your personal vision, it helps to start by reflecting on your noble, highest purpose in life.[8]

My Noble Purpose

Webster's Dictionary defines *noble* as "possessing outstanding qualities, arising from superiority in mind or character." The *Encarta Dictionary* adds, "relating to high moral principles based on high ideals or revealing excellent moral character; magnificent." Add to that the notion of *purpose*: "the reason for which something is done or made."

What is your noble purpose? Reflect on these questions:

- *What impact or contribution have you made by being who you are?*
- *What impact or contribution are you currently making?*
- *What impact or contribution can you make?*

The questions are daunting. But don't get stuck. Open your mind.

Step 1: Generate Possibilities

Write two or three statements about what your noble purpose could be.

1. My noble purpose could be . . .

....

....

....

2. My noble purpose could be . . .

....

....

....

3. My noble purpose could be . . .

....

....

....

My Noble Purpose

Step 2: If I Could, I Would . . .

If I could accomplish one thing in my life, it would be . . .

_____

_____

_____

_____

If I could make an important contribution to my work, it would be . . .

_____

_____

_____

_____

Something I wish I could change in my work is . . .

_____

_____

_____

_____

If I had the power to make any change at all in the world, it would be . . .

_____

_____

_____

_____

My Noble Purpose

Step 3: My Noble Purpose

Review what you have written about what is most important to you. Do you notice a pattern, or one idea that comes up over and over, in different ways? Summarize this pattern or idea in a sentence or two.

My noble purpose is . . .

_____

_____

_____

_____

Why is having a noble purpose compelling? Quite simply, we want our lives to have meaning—we want it to have mattered that we were alive. In the next few pages, you will take this exploration further, focusing on several aspects of your Ideal Self and personal vision. There are four sections, each of which includes a series of exercises:

1. My Dreams and Images of a Desired Future

2. My Passion, Calling, Purpose, and Legacy

3. My Values and Philosophy

4. My Personal Vision

Each of the exercises takes time and reflection. Do not try to rush them. They should provoke somewhat different thoughts and feelings. If you are involved in a loving and caring relationship, you may consider asking your spouse or partner to complete these exercises and questionnaires as both of you explore your personal visions individually and then as a couple or family. You may even want to explore this with your work team or a group of friends.

One note on how to work through the exercises in these sections: the exercises are arranged in an order that helps most people think ever more deeply about what matters most to them. And, each exercise serves a slightly different purpose, even though a few of them look similar. You will find that if you do all of them, you will craft a rich and varied view of your ideal life and future.

My Dreams and Images of a Desired Future

The first step in developing a clear view of your Ideal Self and personal vision is to think big and wide by engaging your dreams and fantasies. Your dreams and fantasies are unique to you and come from a magical combination of your personality, life experiences, and feelings. Five special exercises will add different perspectives to your vision of an ideal future for yourself. The themes or patterns you see will help you construct your personal vision.

27 Things I Want to Do Before I Die

List 27 things you would like to do or experience before you die.

1. _____
2. _____
3. _____
4. _____
5. _____
6. _____
7. _____
8. _____
9. _____
10. _____
11. _____
12. _____
13. _____
14. _____

15. _____
16. _____
17. _____
18. _____
19. _____
20. _____
21. _____
22. _____
23. _____
24. _____
25. _____
26. _____
27. _____

What themes appear in your list?

_____

_____

_____

_____

_____

The Lottery: If I Could, I Would . . .

You just won the super lottery and received 50 million dollars or the equivalent in your currency after tax. How would your life and work change?

My Ideal Life

It is fifteen years from today. You are living your ideal life. You live in a location that you have always dreamed about. You live with the people with whom you most want to be living. If work is part of your ideal life, you are doing the type of work you love, and just enough—not too much, not too little.

Someone videotapes you all day long. What would we see in that video? Where would you be? What are you doing? Who else is there?

My Life in the Year 20__

Project yourself into the future. It is ten years from today. Picture what you most hope your life and work will be on that day.

In 20___, I am ___ years old.

If I am working, my work is best described as ....

....

My major work responsibilities are ....

....

The people I will see or talk to today include ....

....

The people with whom I live and socialize are ....

....

My most important possessions are ....

....

If someone were describing me to a friend today, they would say that I am ....

....

When I have some free time, I spend it ....

....

My leisure or fun activities in a typical week include ....

....

At least once a year, I try to ....

....

....

....

....

My Fantasy Job

This is an opportunity to imagine yourself doing the kind of work that you sometimes wonder about: "What would it be like if I were doing X?"

Make believe that:

1. You enter a new machine called a Neurophysiological Remaker. Using genetic reengineering and noninvasive neural implants, a few minutes inside the machine gives you the body, knowledge, and capability to do any job—and do it well.

2. You have been given the financial resources to do any job you want, and you are free of all personal, social, and financial responsibilities.

List several jobs that you would love to do or try. Consider a wide variety of jobs like those in other countries and jobs in sports, music, medicine, politics, agriculture, and religion. Consider jobs you have heard about or seen in the movies or on television.

....

....

....

....

Choose the three jobs in your list that most interest you or seem the most exciting or rewarding. Describe each of them below, including what you would enjoy or look forward to the most about each job.

1. ....

    ....

2. ....

    ....

3. ....

    ....

My Fantasy Job

Sometimes, a person describes a fantasy job as one he or she really wants to do. Other times, the job represents some interesting or exciting activities or conditions. In other words, sometimes it is not the job that is the fantasy, but some aspect of it or conditions under which the job is done.

As you read your descriptions of the jobs you would most like to do or try, do you notice themes or patterns? How are these different jobs similar? Are there activities (such as being outdoors) that are part of each? Are there conditions of the work (such as working with a team) that are part of each? Are there outcomes (such as being famous) that are part of each? List those themes or patterns below.

Creating Your Dream

The Reverend Martin Luther King Jr. inspired people across the United States and the rest of the world with his "I Have a Dream" speech, which he delivered on August 28, 1963, on the steps of the Lincoln Memorial.[9] His optimistic words resonated in the hearts and minds of millions. Optimism is the mental state in which one's worldview and expectations are generally more positive than negative. Personal optimism correlates strongly with self-esteem, psychological well-being, and personal health.[10] One way to invoke optimism is to imagine what you could be and do. What are your dreams?

I have a dream for myself that . . .

I have a dream that my work will be . . .

I have a dream that my family and children will . . .

I have a dream that my community will . . .

I have a dream that my country will . . .

I have a dream that the world will . . .

Major Themes in My Dreams

Read your statements in the last six exercises. Do you see any themes
or patterns? What are they? What is missing?

My Passion, Calling, Purpose, and Legacy

This section invites exploration of the impact we want to have in life. Articulating the things we are passionate about taps into a deep reservoir of positive emotions, energy, and drive. The exercises "My Legacy," "My Passion," "My Calling," and "What Will People Say About Me?" will help you clarify your dreams and begin to develop a picture of what is most important to you, what you want to do in life, and how you want people to see you.

My Legacy

What do you want your legacy in life to be? In other words, what will remain or continue as a result of your having lived and worked all these years?

My Passion

What am I most committed to in life? What are the things that excite me and make me feel alive, useful, and engaged in meaningful activity and relationships? What issue or cause is an enduring theme in my life?

You may want to write your thoughts here. Or, if you prefer, you can gather pictures from magazines and newspapers and paste them here to form a collage. Or, gather electronic pictures, images, words, and music, and create a personal movie or slide show.

My Calling

If you feel drawn to a particular purpose in life, what is it? If you feel called to fulfill a purpose in life, live a certain way, or make certain contributions, what are they?

What Will People Say About Me?

At your funeral, someone gets up and gives a moving speech that would make you feel warm and proud (if you were there, which of course you are not). What would he or she say about you and your contributions? What feelings does he or she describe in the stories about you? What would you most like the people listening to remember about you?

Ideal Self

Sacrifice & Renewal

Real Self

Mindfulness

Resonant Leadership

Learning Plan

....

....

....

....

....

....

....

....

My Values and Philosophy

The objectives of the "My Values" and "Philosophical Orientation Questionnaire" exercises are to help you clarify your values and beliefs and to give you insight about how these affect your behavior. Our values are based on beliefs. These beliefs have real impact—they determine our attitudes and affect what choices we make in life and how we behave. A value typically includes an evaluation, and sets of values form proscriptions and prescriptions—rules about what *not* to do and what *to do*—that guide our daily life. Values also affect how we interpret and perceive people and events around us and the emotional charge we ascribe to what we see and experience.

Values are influenced by the unique combination of life experiences, significant relationships, social context, and personality that comprises our unique self. Since our values and beliefs change from time to time, after reflection or certain events, it is useful to review and consider our values and beliefs regularly.[11] By taking the time to review and reflect on our values, we can make better, more conscious choices about life, work, and our behavior. As you reflect on the values, beliefs, and personal characteristics that guide you, consider the extent to which you would like these ideals to be part of your daily life.

My Values

Ideal Self

Sacrifice & Renewal

Real Self

Mindfulness

Resonant Leadership

Learning Plan

Beliefs, Principles, and Personal Characteristics That Guide My Life

Below is a list of values, beliefs, or personal characteristics for your consideration. Each of the steps in this process will help you identify which are most important to you and which are guiding principles in your life. It is difficult to choose, of course, because many of these values and characteristics will be at least somewhat important to you. It is also hard to choose because you might find yourself thinking, "I should value X and put it first on my list," even though it really isn't. So, force yourself to choose, and choose based on your true feelings, not the "shoulds" in life.

You might find it useful to determine degrees of importance by imagining how you would feel if you were forced to give up believing in or acting on a particular value, belief, or personal characteristic. Or, think about how you would feel if your life really revolved around certain values, beliefs, or characteristics. How would this make you feel? Sometimes, you might find it helpful to consider two values at a time, asking yourself about the relative importance of one over the other.

1. Start by circling the fifteen or so values that are most important to you.
2. Then, from this list, identify the ten that are the most important to you and write them in a list.
3. From this list of ten, circle the five that are the most important to you.

My Values

List of Values, Beliefs, or Desirable Personal Characteristics

Accomplishment	Control	Independence	Reliable
Achievement	Cooperation	Improving society	Religion
Adventure	Courageous	Innovative	Respectful
Affection	Courteous	Integrity	Responsible
Affectionate	Creativity	Intellectual	Restrained
Affiliation	Dependable	Involvement	Salvation
Ambitious	Disciplined	Imagination	Self-controlled
Assisting others	Economic security	Joy	Self-reliance
Authority	Effective	Leisurely	Self-respect
Autonomy	Equality	Logical	Sincerity
Beauty	Excitement	Love	Spirituality
Belonging	Fame	Loving	Stability
Broad-minded	Family happiness	Mature love	Status
Caring	Family security	National security	Success
Challenge	Forgiving	Nature	Symbolic
Cheerful	Free choice	Obedient	Taking risks
Clean	Freedom	Order	Teamwork
Comfortable life	Friendship	Peace	Tidy
Companionship	Fun	Personal development	Tender
Compassion	Genuineness	Pleasure	Tranquility
Competent	Happiness	Polite	Wealth
Competitiveness	Health	Power	Winning
Contribution to others	Helpfulness	Pride	Wisdom
Conformity	Honesty	Rational	Others:
Contentedness	Hope	Recognition	

My Ten Most Important Values

1. ....
2. ....
3. ....
4. ....
5. ....

6. ....
7. ....
8. ....
9. ....
10. ....

Finally, rank each of your five most important values, beliefs, or characteristics, with "1" being the most important value to you, to "5" being the least important of these five important values.

1. ....
2. ....
3. ....

4. ....
5. ....

"My Values" is not an easy exercise. Most people find the first step easy, but the last step difficult, even uncomfortable. That is because the reflection forces us to reconcile a number of potentially divergent aspects of our current lives. When you develop the final list of five values and rank-order them, you inevitably keep asking yourself, "Does this placement of the value reflect how I act or how I would like to act?" In other words, does the ranking of the value represent the person you are today in your actions and decisions? If it does not, then does it represent the person you would like to become? You might also wonder, "Does the placement of the value in the ranking reflect my current preferences, attitudes, actions, and decisions? Or does it better reflect the way I was a few years ago—a past, earlier me?"

Our Personal Philosophy

Understanding our values becomes a moral rudder, helping us steer through confusing and sometimes conflicting moments and decisions. But our specific values do not always explain all our actions. For example, two managers attending an executive education class both listed "family" as their number one value. One executive chose to be a vice president of a large international company and flew to another city every Sunday night or Monday morning. He returned to his home each Friday night or Saturday morning. The other executive, a plant manager of a chemical company, had turned down two promotions in the last year—one position because it would involve a lot of travel and the other because it would have required his family to move. When asked how each of them could place "family" in the same position of importance and yet have such different lifestyles and choices, the men gave very different answers about *how* they enacted their value for family.

The VP said that he valued his family and that it showed in how he provided for them. His wife had the home she always wanted and the freedom to pursue a job that did not pay much but was one that she loved. His children went to the best private schools, and their financial future was secure.

The plant manager said that putting his family first meant "I get home for dinner with my family six nights a week. We spend time together doing whatever families do or, more importantly, what we want to do."

There are two possible ways to understand this dichotomy. One explanation is that at least one executive was unaware of his actions and their impact on others. We knew each of the men well, and this did not seem to be the case—both men constantly weighed their decisions according to how those decisions would affect their families. The second possibility was that the difference was not in what they valued; it was in *how they manifested their values.* This is a person's *operating philosophy:* a set of beliefs that drives choices about how to act on one's values. In other words, while the two men placed high value on family, their operating philosophies guided their choices about how they acted in relation to their families. In the following pages, you can use the "Philosophical Orientation Questionnaire" to understand how you choose to take action.

Philosophical Orientation Questionnaire[a]

How I Enact My Values[a]

This instrument includes twenty sets of choices. For each of the twenty items, consider the choices given and indicate your current preference within each item by giving each a score of 1, 2, or 3.

The option ranked "1" should be your first choice; the option ranked "2" should be your second choice; and the option ranked "3" should be your last choice. Some of the choices have multiple parts, separated by "*or.*" For these, select the part of the choice you most like, underline it, and assign the rank for that item while disregarding other parts of the item.

1. **I think of my value, or worth, in terms of**

   a .... My relationships (e.g., family, friends)

   b .... My ideas or ability to invent new concepts *or* ability to analyze things

   c .... My financial net worth *or* income

2. **I feel most proud of organizations to which I belong when they**

   a .... Have created new products/services

   b .... Create financial worth for individuals (regardless of whether the people are employees, investors, or partners) *or* create jobs

   c .... Have helped people live easier and healthier lives

3. **When someone asks me to commit to spending time on a project, I ask myself**

   a .... What can I learn from doing it?

   b .... Will it help someone, or is someone counting on me to do it?

   c .... Is it worth it to me?

4. **Sometimes I will do something for no other reason than because**

   a .... I want to figure out why something works the way it does

   b .... It has to be done in order to do something else *or* get something I want

   c .... It will allow me to be with a person I care about *or* it would please someone I care about

5. The way I can best contribute to others' lives is to

a........ Help them find jobs *or* develop financial security and independence

b........ Help them develop principles with which to guide their lives

c........ Help them build relationships with others or me *or* help them feel better about themselves

6. I get the most done when I am with someone I would describe as

a........ Pragmatic

b........ Caring

c........ Analytic

7. I consider my contribution to society in terms of

a........ Ideas, concepts, or products

b........ Money

c........ People and relationships

8. I define myself in terms of

a........ What I accomplish *or* what I do (i.e., my activity/behavior)

b........ My thoughts, values, and ideas

c........ The people with whom I have relationships

9. I would describe myself as

a........ Analytic

b........ Caring

c........ Pragmatic

10. I consider the most important stakeholders of the organization for whom I work to be

a........ The field or industry of which we are a part

b........ The employees

c........ The shareholders/investors *or* the customers/clients

Philosophical Orientation Questionnaire

11. **When I read or listen to the news, I often think about**

   a .... Whether it gives me an idea as to how to make money *or* seize an opportunity

   b .... The statement/s it makes about the nature of our society

   c .... The people in the stories (i.e., those affected by the events)

12. **I believe many of society's problems could be resolved if more people were**

   a .... Pragmatic

   b .... Analytic

   c .... Caring

13. **When I have free time, I prefer to**

   a .... Do things that need to be done (e.g., chores, duties)

   b .... Figure out things *or* think about what, why, and how things work and are the way they are

   c .... Spend time talking and doing things with specific other people

14. **The following are good principles to live by**

   a .... Don't put off until tomorrow what you can do today

   b .... Do unto others as you would have others do unto you

   c .... To contemplate the meaning of life and events is an important activity

15. **I have the most fun, stimulation, or excitement when I am with someone whom I describe as**

   a .... Pragmatic

   b .... Caring

   c .... Analytic

16. I feel that an organization should contribute to society by

a .... Providing a place for people to realize their dreams, develop, and contribute

b .... Creating ideas, products, or services

c .... Creating increased net worth (i.e., helping individuals build their net worth) or creating jobs

17. People have spent a full life if they have

a .... Cared for others and built relationships

b .... Made a lot of money or achieved financial security or created jobs

c .... Developed ideas, products, or methods

18. Individuals should

a .... Identify their goals and then work toward them, making sacrifices when necessary for their long term goals

b .... Seek fulfillment through their relationships

c .... Understand themselves and why they do things

19. I will feel successful if, in ten years, I have

a .... Written articles/books or taught people ideas, concepts or invented new concepts, ideas, products or have figured a number of things out

b .... Known many people well or a number of meaningful relationships

c .... A greater net worth than I do now or financial security and freedom

20. My time is well spent in an activity if

a .... I make friends or meet interesting people

b .... I get interesting ideas or observations from it

c .... I can make money from the activity

Philosophical Orientation Questionnaire

Scoring the Questionnaire

To calculate your scores on the Philosophical Orientation Questionnaire:

1. Copy the number you placed next to each item in the questionnaire to the right of that item on the chart on the next page.
2. Add all the items in each column for a column subtotal.
3. Subtract the subtotal of each column from 60 to obtain a score for Pragmatic Value, Intellectual Value, and Human Value. Because you ranked the most important item from each question with a "1," your scores have to be reversed and subtracted from a maximum score of 60 to generate a number for which a high score means a stronger operating philosophy.

Your highest score, after you subtract it from 60, is the operating philosophy you use most frequently in making decisions, determining the value and worth of things and activities.

Philosophical Orientation Questionnaire

Item Numbers from Questionnaire	Pragmatic Value	Intellectual Value	Human Value
	1 c	1 b	1 a
	2 b	2 a	2 c
	3 c	3 a	3 b
	4 b	4 a	4 c
	5 a	5 b	5 c
	6 a	6 c	6 b
	7 b	7 a	7 c
	8 a	8 b	8 c
	9 c	9 a	9 b
	10 c	10 a	10 b
	11 a	11 b	11 c
	12 a	12 b	12 c
	13 a	13 b	13 c
	14 a	14 c	14 b
	15 a	15 c	15 b
	16 c	16 b	16 a
	17 b	17 c	17 a
	18 a	18 c	18 b
	19 c	19 a	19 b
	20 c	20 b	20 a
Add the scores			
Subtract from 60 for your **total**			

Philosophical Orientation Questionnaire

Interpretation of the Philosophical Orientation Questionnaire

This questionnaire is designed to assist you in exploring your preferences regarding three basic operating philosophies: Pragmatic, Intellectual, and Human. Through a mixture of these three philosophies, you manifest your values. People see the worth, benefit, or goodness in ourselves, others, and organizations through the lens of our dominant operating philosophy.

Pragmatic Operating Philosophy

A Pragmatic Operating Philosophy appears to be based in philosophies of utilitarianism, pragmatism, or consequentialism. When the Pragmatic Operating Philosophy dominates, a person will tend to determine the worthiness of an activity in terms of its utility in helping achieve desired ends. When the ends or objectives are not clear, or if it is difficult to measure outcomes, the activity will be less valued by those with a high score. A note of caution: although money provides a convenient measure for many work-related outcomes, a strong Pragmatic Operating Philosophy does not imply that a person is preoccupied with financial gain. Money may merely be one measure he or she uses to value an activity. Other measures of cost versus benefit are also common but may be more subtle.

Intellectual Operating Philosophy

An Intellectual Operating Philosophy appears to be based in a philosophy of rationalism and possibly in the abstractions of mysticism. A person whose dominant operating philosophy is Intellectual will tend to determine the worthiness of an activity in terms of its conceptual contribution to understanding something. Creating a cognitive map, or a framework describing what we know about something, is at the heart of what is important to people whose dominant operating philosophy is Intellectual. There is a tendency to value and use abstract and symbolic variables to understand, describe, or explore life, relationships, and activities.

Human Operating Philosophy

A Human Operating Philosophy appears to be based in philosophies of humanism and communitarianism. With a dominant Human Operating Philosophy, a person will tend to determine the worthiness of an activity in terms of its affect on specific other people and its impact on the quality of the relationship he or she has with specific

Philosophical Orientation Questionnaire

others. Intimacy and friendship—at home and at work—may be of primary importance to someone whose dominant operating philosophy is Human.

What Do My Scores Mean?

Everyone tends to have a dominant operating philosophy, although of course each of us believes in all three philosophies to some degree. Many people will believe one of these philosophies is more important than the others at certain points in their lives, and the relative importance of the three operating philosophies may change over time.

Begin your interpretation of your responses to this questionnaire by asking yourself if the total scores reflect your personal beliefs about the relative importance or ranking of these three operating philosophies.

The gap between the various scores may reflect the strength of your preference for the operating philosophies. If any of your scores are close together, say, within three points, it could mean that you feel conflicted when making certain types of decisions. You may even feel indecisive.

This isn't necessarily the case, however, as you can see by looking at your scores another way. This time, you will plot your scores on a percentile chart. On the chart, find the point on each of the three percentile graphs to place your total score. Connect the three dots to form a line.[b]

The raw scores and the percentile distribution are both helpful, but in different ways. The raw scores reflect how you answered each question. The percentile distribution compares your scores with those of other people who completed the questionnaire. The percentile chart is said to adjust for the distortion resulting from the social desirability or political correctness of certain answers. Since both the raw scores and the percentile graph provide slightly different information, you should analyze both for insights into your operating philosophy.

For example, suppose that after subtracting from 60 your Pragmatic Operating Philosophy score was 12, your Intellectual Operating Philosophy score was 24, and your human operating philosophy score was 24. Because the raw scores of the Intellectual and Human Operating Philosophies are close, it suggests that you may feel internal

Philosophical Orientation Questionnaire

conflict at times when a situation involves people you care about and issues of justice, fairness, or adherence to procedures. But when placed on the percentile chart, your percentile scores become 34 for Pragmatic, 82 for Intellectual, and 43 for Human. This means that when others see how you act in many situations or over time, they would see that you would more frequently try to understand situations, create models or frameworks that explain what is going on rather than thinking about other people's feelings (the Human Operating Philosophy) or calculating the costs and benefits of one versus another option (the Pragmatic Operating Philosophy). It does not mean that you do not care about people, nor does it mean that you are not pragmatic. It is a relative weight.

a. © 1992 by Richard Boyatzis. For in-depth reading about the test and its theoretical base as well as statistical reliability and validity, see Richard E. Boyatzis, Angela Murphy, and Jane Wheeler, "Philosophy As the Missing Link Between Values and Behavior," *Psychological Reports* 86, no. 1 (2000): 47–64.

b. Philosophical Orientation Questionnaire percentiles: The profile reflects a percentile distribution of your scores using the total score against 1,320 managers, executives, and professionals. This sample has a range of 17 to 63, with an average age of 32. It is just over one-third female and comes from U.S., European, South American, and Asian samples.

Philosophical Orientation Questionnaire

Percentile	Pragmatic 30+	Intellectual 32+	Human 38+
100%			
98	29	31	37
96	28	30	35
94	26	28	34
92	24	27	33
90%	23	26	32
	22	25	
	21		
	20	24	31
80%			30
	19	23	
	18	22	
			29
70%			
	17	21	28
			27
60%	16	20	
			26
	15		
50%		19	25
	14		
		18	24
	13		
40%		17	23
	12		
			22
		16	
30%		15	21
	11		20
		14	
20%	10		19
			18
	9	13	
			17
	8	12	16
10%	7	11	15
		10	14
	6	9	
	5	8	12

Living Values

Now let's look at how we enact our values in relation to other people and in different spheres of our life. The "Circles of Life" exercise will help you take stock of the relative value you place on important areas of your life.

Circles of Life

In the Circles of Life below are words that represent areas of life that are typically important to people. What areas of life are most important to you?

Draw a set of circles for yourself, and write words to describe your valued Circles of Life. You might choose to use circle size and proximity to indicate how important they are and how they fit together.

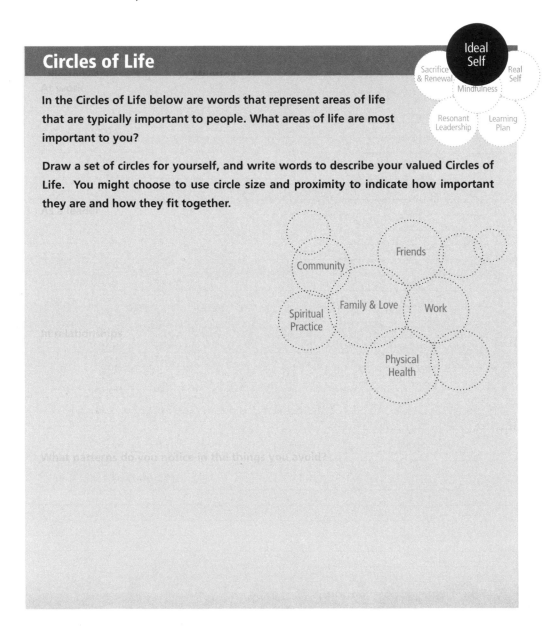

My Personal Vision

It is now time to pull together all these reflections into a coherent statement of your desired future in an essay, "My Personal Vision." This vision for your desired life will serve as your starting point for a learning plan. As you write your Personal Vision, you will probably find inspiration, energy, optimism, and a compelling path to your future.

Although the essay can take many forms, we recommend that you begin with a brief statement and overview of what you want in your future. This might be one or two paragraphs, and it should incorporate enough specificity for a reader to know what you hope for and what your dreams are. Then, expand your thoughts. Write fully about what you desire, considering all aspects of life that are important to you. To be most useful to you, the complete essay should be at least two or three pages in length.

Extend the vision for as long as you wish. It could be five to seven years, ten to fifteen years, or twenty-five years from now. Using your reflections in the previous exercises, explain the elements of this dream of the future, making sure to cover topics such as these: *What would my ideal life and work be in the period I'm thinking about? What will I be doing then? Where will I be? Who will be with me? What will my work and life be like? What or who will I be?* Make sure you cover your physical health; your family, friends, the rest of your community, and society (including your contributions to all these groups); and your spiritual life.

My Personal Vision

Ideal
Self

Sacrifice
& Renewal

Real
Self

Mindfulness

Resonant
Leadership

Learning
Plan

My Personal Vision

Congratulations! You now have a picture of the future you desire. In the next chapter, you will conduct an honest appraisal of your roles, identities, strengths, and weaknesses so that you know more about yourself and what you have to work with in attaining that future.

Chapter 5

APPRECIATING YOUR REAL SELF

Seeing the Whole Picture

JILL HU HAD JUST BEEN NAMED Vice President of consumer relations for a *Fortune* 100 apparel company.[1] She was excited by the opportunity to take her leadership to a new level. The challenges were real—the matrix structure was complex and the relational landscape complicated. Jill was eager and confident, but like most people facing a big change, she was just a bit anxious about the new role. Could she hit the ground running? Could she do the job without compromising her family life? She loved being a mother and wife, and she didn't want these roles to suffer as she took on new responsibilities.

We met Jill on a sunny afternoon in Miami, Florida, a few weeks later. She described her excitement about the new position and a vague concern about what she might need to do, learn, and change to manage her new responsibilities. She wasn't quite sure how to do it, but she wanted to get some concrete information and insight about how to lead and about what people saw as her strengths and challenges as a leader.

Over the next few months, Jill spent time articulating her personal vision, going through a very similar process to what you experienced in chapter 4. She reflected on her current leadership situation, her previous work and family experiences, how she enacted her personal values, and what she wanted her leadership to look and feel like in this new situation. Then, we worked with Jill to solicit concrete, real feedback from a few people. We conducted confidential interviews of the nine people Jill had asked to talk with us. These people contributed their perspectives on Jill's strengths and challenges and described what it was like to work with her. The insights from these conversations were analyzed for themes related to Jill's strengths and challenges and the expectations people had of her.

Then we shared these themes directly with Jill. Hearing the perspective of others was liberating for her. Like many successful, achievement-oriented people, Jill had a tendency to dwell on her shortcomings, believing that this approach to change was the best way to achieve the excellence she sought. She ignored or downplayed her strengths. The feedback she received did point out a few things she needed to work on, but the people around her saw far more strengths than weaknesses. This feedback grounded her. She could free herself from her own imagination—she now knew what people thought and felt, and much of what they saw in her gave her a feeling of hope and confidence.

With the help of this feedback and reflection, Jill took an inventory of her current personal and leadership strengths and challenges. She painted a picture of her *Real Self.* This picture was, in her view and ours, fairly accurate. It allowed Jill to clearly see the gaps between who she hoped to be as a leader and a person and who she was today. It also enabled her to see how she might leverage some of her key strengths as a powerful way to step into her new job. And through the process, she also realized that somehow she had lost touch with an important part of life, one that used to provide a source of renewal and inspiration.

In years past, Jill had played classical guitar every day, even playing professionally with a group of friends in a quartet. And although she had played music regularly for more than twenty years, when she got caught up in adult life, she simply stopped. Midway though our work together, she went out and bought a new guitar and began playing again. After a few weeks, she was playing almost every evening, sometimes by herself and sometimes with her kids. It was easy to start again, and her playing brought great joy to Jill and her family. Her enjoyment of the guitar, a characteristic of her true and essential self, was a profound gift of renewal, a treasured activity that she recovered and reintegrated into her life with great results.

Why do we raise this particular change in Jill's life, one that might seem small and not linked to her professional life? Profound personal change and leadership development are almost always linked to looking at one's current life holistically. In other words, there is something about examining balance, and by this, we don't just mean comparing how much time you spend at work with how much you spend at home. People who want real change will need to look at *all* aspects of their lives, not just leadership skills. For Jill, realizing that she had lost something that truly gave her joy—music—was a wake-up call.

Resonant leaders like Jill have an accurate sense of themselves; this sense includes clear insight about what they are good at, what is difficult for them, and what they need to learn and do in life to be at their best. Effective change involves mindful awareness of *who you currently are.* We each have unique characteristics that form as a result of our biology, life experiences, and current situation. We are always evolving and adapting as we encounter new situations in life. When we get a new job, enter into new relationships, or leave old ones, small or even big changes can occur. In this chapter, you will explore who you are today. You will have a chance to become more mindful as you navigate your evolution as a person and a leader.[2]

Let's begin by taking stock of where you are today and consider your strengths and challenges. This assessment, coupled with your

Personal Vision, will allow you to build a learning and development plan that will help you realize your vision and maintain the parts of it you are already living.

You will start by looking at what seems to be working and what seems to be out of synch for you at work and at home. You will reflect on past and current roles that influence how you live and lead. You will also catalog your strengths—qualities you can build on to become more effective. You may also identify potential weaknesses, challenges, and gaps that you need to address. And, because people don't work and live completely alone, you will take stock of key relationships and explore how the people closest to you factor into your leadership and learning journey.

I Am Who I Am
How Have I Become the Person I Am Today?

Who you are is a combination of how you regularly act (the things you feel, do, and say); your experiences, roles, and identity; and your dreams, values, and beliefs. In the earlier chapters, you explored your beliefs and dreams. Now you explore how you act—that is, what you actually do, how you see yourself, and how others see you. We are all influenced by our experiences. Here is a series of exercises to help you see patterns over the entire course of your life. These exercises will take you on a reflective journey back to the past. They will help you explore your life in depth, including various emotionally engaging experiences. By conjuring up these stories and the emotions within, you will begin a reflective process of seeing yourself as you really are. You can start by looking at who you are today. As you look at pictures of who you really are, you probably notice that you have changed over the course of your life. As you do the

Pictures of Me

Look through your photo library and find a few pictures that show the "real you." Paste them here. Look at them carefully. What is it about these pictures that show who you really are?

next few exercises, you will become more aware of lessons you have learned from your experiences, and understand what you are passionate about. By focusing on times when you felt the happiest and the most emotionally alive, as well as on times that were difficult, the exercises will help you better understand yourself. This process is a powerful reminder of how you have grown and changed and how crucial it is to pay attention to the most important aspects of your life.

My Lifeline

How Did I Get Here?

On the following page, draw a long line, straight or curved. On the far left, write the year you were born. On the far right, note today's date and finish the line with an arrow pointing to the future.

On your lifeline, write:

- Important events such as school graduations, job beginnings and endings, the birth of a child, the death of a loved one, and the beginning or ending of important relationships, etc.
- Transition phases—times that now, with the wisdom of perspective, you can see that you were in transition
- Personal high points and times when you struggled
- Moments or accomplishments of which you are proud and those you are sorry for or have regret about

Include both personal and professional events. Review your emotional journey, and include times when you felt happiest and most engaged with life, as well as times when you felt more or less lost, sad, or confused. Be sure to pay attention to the emotions you felt then and those you feel now as you remember and write.

Sharing Your Lifeline

"My Lifeline" is a great exercise to do with a work group, a study group, friends, or a loved one. When people do this together, they tend to have deeper personal insights, they build trusting relationships that are more authentic. If you want to use this exercise with a group, have all the participants reflect and write by themselves first, and then come together and tell each other—one at a time—the stories of their lives.

As each person tells his or her story, others should listen quietly. People may wish to ask a question for clarification, or share what is evoked in them as they listen to the story. It works best, though, if each person speaks without a lot of interruptions. Close the group with a discussion of common themes and talk about what each person learned from the exercise.

Patterns of Change

We get additional information about the progress of our life from looking at the rhythm of changes we have made. The "Rhythms of My Career" and "Transitions in Life and Work" exercises will help you do this.

Rhythms of My Career

Starting with your *current* job or role, write your title or brief description of your role at the top of the ladder. Beside it, write the date when you made the transition into this job or role and highlights of the experience. Then in the next rung down the ladder, write the job or role you held previously, then the date when you entered that job or role and highlights of that experience. Complete the ladder backwards in time from the present to the point at which you first started working, took a job or assumed adult responsibilities. Please include all work and roles that you consider meaningful, including significant part-time or unpaid work and work in the home, such as raising children.

Rhythms of My Career

My current Job
Transition date and
highlights of the experience

The job before that
Transition date and highlights
of the experience

The job before that
Transition date and highlights
of the experience

My first job

After noting your jobs and transitions, examine the number of years between major changes. A major change is not necessarily every job change or even organization change, but one that means you began approaching work and life differently.

Do you notice a rhythm in your cycle of interest and boredom in work? If so, where are you in the current cycle?

Rhythms of My Career

Now look at the number of years between the major life events you recalled and recorded on your Lifeline and compare it to the time periods in between important changes in your career. Is there a pattern to when you feel the need for a change or when changes seem to occur? If so, where are you *today* in the current rhythm?

....

....

....

....

....

....

....

Transitions are very special times. They are times of uncertainty and emergence. Out of transition, new forms emerge. It's important to understand your typical way of going through transitions so that you can increase your self-awareness and potentially change your process of transitions. The exercise "Transitions in Life and at Work" will help you understand this important aspect of how you approach work and life.

Transitions in Life and at Work

Select a few important transitions from the two previous exercises. Briefly describe each transition and then write a few notes about who or what helped you make progress, as well as who or what inhibited your progress through the transition.

Transition #1 ....

....

....

Transition #2 ....

....

....

Transition #3 ....

....

....

Transition #4 ....

....

....

What patterns do you see? Consider frequency, duration of the phase, emotional reactions during that time, impact on your key relationships, how you entered, and how you emerged. Did you tend to initiate the transitions or were your transitions inspired by others? Are there any other interesting patterns?

....

....

....

Social Identity and Roles

Another aspect of who you are is tied to the groups to which you belong, the roles you hold, and the relative importance you place on various aspects of your social identity. As mentioned in chapter 4, the beliefs we hold play a very important role in driving our behavior and our perception of others. Our beliefs arise from the groups to which we belong (sometimes called reference groups) and the society in which we live. Our social context has an enormous impact on our beliefs, actions, self-image, and image in others' eyes. The next few exercises will help you clarify your social identity groups and roles and the impact they have on your Real Self.

We travel this world with various social identities—aspects that are not personality based, but formed by the social world in which we live. Some of these identities are based on where and how we grew up. Examples are regional or national identities, social class distinctions, and shared family characteristics. Some social identities emerge from physiological characteristics such as gender, age, race, physical ability, and size. Social identities that we are born with and those that are imposed on us often direct our self-image and behavior in profound ways.

Our social roles and identities shift throughout our lives. They can emerge from roles we have chosen and stages in our lives. For example, we do not take on roles related to parenthood until we are acting as parents. Our profession, our positions in our communities or places of worship, and our membership in political parties can become core to our self-image and they can also change. Sometimes, who we are includes roles or expectations that people have placed on us—roles such as *boss*, *friend*, and *oldest child*. These may or may not be aligned with our core values or self-image, but can nonetheless have great impact on our strengths, our choices, and the challenges we face in our communities, at work, and in life. Taken all together, our social identities and roles form a prism through which we view the world and it views us.

Most of the time, we take our social identities and roles more or less for granted. We don't spend much time considering how they affect our feelings, thoughts, behavior, and way of life. But social roles and identities, whether chosen or imposed, greatly influence what we believe we can be or can accomplish in life. To fully understand ourselves, we must examine how we fit into the social fabric of our organizations, communities, and families.

This is even more important for leaders, because the higher you go in an organizational hierarchy, the more your role affects how people treat you and what they expect of you. While you may feel like a normal person, others see you as exalted, or demonic, or both. People are more likely to treat you as a role than as a person. So understanding and owning your roles allows you to manage your own expectations and to understand others' treatment of you. The purpose of the next exercise is to help heighten your awareness of the various social roles and identities you currently hold and to explore how they affect your own and others' expectations and perceptions of you.

My Social Identities and Roles

Ideal Self

Sacrifice & Renewal

Real Self

Mindful

Resonant Leadership

Learning Plan

Part 1: Start the process of exploring your social identities by filling in this chart. As you do so, think about which aspects of your identity are chosen, which you were born with, or which feel imposed on you. Also consider how society's view of your different identities affects how you think of yourself and how you behave.

Race ....

Ethnicity ....

Gender ....

Religion ....

Sexual Orientation ....

Physical Characteristics

....

Political Affiliation ....

National Identity ....

Profession ....

Regional Affiliation ....

Social Class ....

Language ....

Defining Physical Characteristics ......

....

Hobby and Leisure Interests............

Birth Order ....

Other ....

Part 2: List as many of your social roles as you can (e.g., mother, brother, vice president, civil engineer, board member, etc.)

My Social Identities and Roles

Part 3: How Social Identities and Roles Affect Me Now

Which roles and social identities are most important to you? Why?

How were you taught about your identities?

Are there any aspects of your identity or roles that you are interested in exploring more deeply? Which ones and why?

My Social Identities and Roles

How has your sense of the relative importance of your various social identities changed over the course of your life? In what ways?

....

....

....

....

....

....

Have there been particular jobs or organizations that heightened your experience of your different social identities and roles? How?

....

....

....

....

....

....

My Social World

Very few humans live without relationships. Like most other mammals, we are a social species—our relationships help shape who we are. Our work lives are filled with many kinds of relationships—bosses, peers, colleagues, people who work for us, suppliers, customers, and many others. Our lives are filled with other kinds of important relationships: family, neighbors, our children's teachers, friends, service providers, and on and on. Each of these relationships has its own music, feel, needs, expectations, benefits, and challenges.

The relational world in which we currently live and work helps determine the power of how we experience our social roles and identities. And, by extension, the context in which we live influences how we experience ourselves. This next section will invite you to take an inventory of your social world—who is in it, your relationships, and how these relationships support and challenge you.

Relationships provide and demand energy. The next exercise, "My Social Web," will help you take stock of your current relationships.

My Social Web

Ideal Self
Sacrifice & Renewal
Real Self
Mindful
Resonant Leadership
Learning Plan

Where Do I Belong?

The purpose of this exercise is to help you see the variety and number of relationships you have, to reflect on the characteristics of these relationships and consider if you are getting and giving what you want within them.

Put your name in the middle of the Social Web on the following page. Now, think of the key relationships you have in your life and at work.

From your name, draw a line out and write "Family." From "Family" draw lines and write the names of the key family members who you actively and frequently relate to. No need to write them all down: just indicate relationships that require your energy and demand your active participation. Mark each relationship line for your sense of whether the relationship is currently resonant (+) or dissonant (–).

Now go back to the center (your name) and draw lines out for your direct reports and write their names. Do the same for your key work relationships, your key customer relationships, key peers, and your boss(es). If you want to make this even more elaborate, consider the family members of your key associates, and the associates of your associates, etc. Finally, draw a line or lines and write the names of other people or groups with whom you are in deep relationship. This is likely to include friends and community members. Depending on where you are in life, you might include your doctor, a coach, a spiritual teacher or counselor. Be sure to mark all your relationship lines as resonant (+) or dissonant (–).

Example of a Social Web

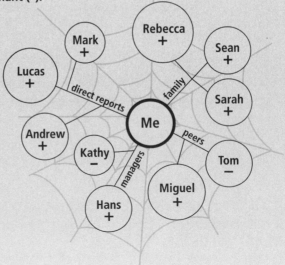

My Social Web

What My Social Web Means to Me

Notice your emotional reactions as you look at your social web. Write notes in the space below about the thoughts or emotional reactions you are experiencing.

What patterns do you see?

_____

_____

_____

Do an emotional scan of the web: are there any warm or cold areas?

_____

_____

_____

Which relationships are harmonious?

_____

_____

_____

Which relationships are more stressful?

_____

_____

_____

What do you notice about where you expend your energy?

_____

_____

_____

My Social Web

Which relationships give you energy?

....

....

....

Which relationships drain energy?

....

....

....

Which relationships could provide important feedback and perspective for you?

....

....

....

Do you have unfinished business with anyone?

....

....

....

List the three relationships most in need of your attention.

1. ....

2. ....

3. ....

My Social Web

To take this one step further, you can spend a few minutes jotting some notes about the people on your web. What are their key strengths and gifts? Their unique perspectives? What do they care most about? As you think of them compassionately, what comes to mind? What do your thoughts make you want to do with them? Who sees you as truly important in his or her life? How could you help this other person by being more responsive to his or her needs even if it isn't a high priority for you?

_____

_____

_____

_____

_____

_____

_____

_____

As you review the exercises so far, you can probably see how people and relationships have played a huge part in your life and development. We are shaped and influenced by our relationships. As you consider your life and career, what special people come to mind? How have you been touched by key people in your life? Who has stimulated your growth? What resonant leaders have you known, and how have even dissonant leaders catalyzed your growth? The exercise "A Letter from My Heart" will help you integrate your review of your past and support your reflection about how relationships have helped shape you as a person and a leader.

A Letter from My Heart

Ideal Self · Sacrifice & Renewal · Mindfulness · Real Self · Resonant Leadership · Learning Plan

Most of us have been touched deeply by a few important people: people who, because of their feelings for us and their actions, have helped us to become who we are today. Some of what these special people gave to us was uplifting and inspiring. Sometimes what they gave to us caused pain and only made sense later.

Who has been a very special person in your life? Who has shaped you and helped you to be who you are today?

Write a letter to this person. Tell the person what he or she has done for you, the impact the person has had, and your feelings about how he or she has touched you. Be as honest and authentic as possible. Write from your heart. You may decide later to send this letter, but this first version should be for you.

Who Am I Today? Strengths and Gaps

Now that you have reviewed the past in a few ways and considered your present social world, let's look at how others see you as a person and a leader—who you are today in others' eyes. Assessing your Real Self is so important, you will approach the task in a number of ways, including several self-assessments and structured processes to gather feedback from others and inventories of your current strengths and challenges.

Let's start with your strengths. Why? When you are leading from your strengths, you are tapping into the power of the Positive Emotional Attractor. When you consider your strengths and the positive feedback you will receive, you will feel hopeful, strong, and good about yourself. Enhancing your awareness of your strengths will empower you to manage yourself through the sometimes unsettling work of facing up to the need for change or to your disconnect with your deepest values.

Strengths I See in Myself

Ideal Self · Sacrifice & Renewal · Mindful · **Real Self** · Resonant Leadership · Learning Plan

Strengths can be elements that you were born with, or things you have learned. They are extremely valuable or useful abilities, assets or qualities. What are your strengths? What do you consider your character assets?

Complete this sentence: I am a person who . . .

....

....

Strengths I See in Myself

List ten strengths that have served you well and of which you are most proud. For each strength, notice the sensations or feelings that come up for you as you write it down and reflect on your successes.

My Strengths   Sensations/Feelings

1. ....

2. ....

3. ....

4. ....

5. ....

6. ....

7. ....

8. ....

9. ....

10. ....

Do any of these sensations or feelings surprise you? Why do these things stand out to you? How do these strengths relate to the core values you explored in chapter 4?

....

....

....

....

....

Strengths I See in Myself

Summarize what you consider to be your most important personal and leadership strengths. These elements are likely to be things that you enjoy about yourself and others like about you. They are positive energizers for you.

Strengths Others See in Me

List a few strengths you believe other people see in you. These are the things people tell you you're good at.

At home

At work

Strengths Others See in Me

As a leader

....

....

....

In relationships

....

....

....

How similar were your responses in "Strengths I See in Myself" and "Strengths Others See in Me"? Are the strengths you see in yourself similar to what you believe other people see in you? Places where there are gaps between how you see yourself and how others see you may be areas ripe for you to change, learn new things, or amplify your use of your strengths. These gaps are not necessarily weaknesses, but are areas that may indicate a lack of self-awareness and, as such, may get in the way of your achieving your ideal. As we change and grow, we obviously need to learn new things. Sometimes, what we need to develop exists within us, but we underutilize it or avoid engaging in certain behaviors. We usually do this when we feel less confident or when we haven't found a way to enjoy ourselves when enacting certain skills. Sometimes, we are worried that our behavior will hurt others or be seen as out of character for us. The "Activities and Situations I Tend to Avoid" exercise invites you to think deeply about this aspect of yourself.

Activities and Situations I Tend to Avoid

Ideal Self · Sacrifice & Renewal · Real Self · Mindful · Resonant Leadership · Learning Plan

List a few activities and situations you stay away from:

At home

At work

As a leader

In relationships

What patterns do you notice in the things you avoid?

Activities and Situations I Tend to Avoid

Are there things you avoid in one area of your life (home, work, as a leader, in close relationships), but are able to face and engage with in other areas?

....

....

....

....

....

....

But What Do Others *Really* See in Me?

Up to this point, you have conducted a self-assessment—an audit of where you see yourself in life, your characteristics, what is important to you, and what you believe others see in you. The next exercise, "Leadership Self-Study," invites you to reach out and systematically gather input and perspective from people who know you. This is a crucial step in discovering your Real Self.

We have internal mechanisms that can prevent us from seeing things that may be harmful to us. That's because we have built-in protection, called *ego defense mechanisms.* These help us function and interact with others, but they can also create distortions in our perceptions and patterns of interacting.[3] Seeing ourselves as others see us is difficult because of these distortions. Add to that the creeping mindlessness that can happen when we are trapped in the Sacrifice Syndrome, and we can develop a self-image that is more fantasy than reality.

Because of ego defense mechanisms and our habitual patterns of interaction with others—patterns that develop over a lifetime—it is easy to avoid looking at aspects of ourselves that make us uncomfortable or do not fit our self-image. Oddly enough, we are often just as unwilling to look at our strengths as we are to see our weaknesses. Outside perspective helps in developing a clear view of our strengths as well as our blind spots.

Many people are exposed to a 360-degree feedback process in their work organizations. The idea is that with a questionnaire, you ask your boss, a group of peers, a group of subordinates or direct reports, and sometimes a group of customers or clients, a loved one, and friends to assess how frequently they see you engaging in certain behaviors. This is a highly effective method of collecting a great deal of data from many people and getting a picture of how you interact from other people's experience of you. There are a number of such instruments available on the market, but their accuracy in measuring the behaviors they ask about varies widely. It is important to insure that any questionnaire you use has been properly validated and is a sound instrument. One such well-researched instrument is the Emotional and Social Competency Inventory (ESCI), by Richard Boyatzis and Daniel Goleman.[4]

An alternative to the questionnaire-based process is a 360-degree interview assessment, in which the interviewer talks directly with a number of people about your capabilities. While the questionnaire-based process collects information from many people (often as many as ten to twenty) and helps you compare their responses, interviews provide a depth of information that a survey cannot. But they also take a great deal more time. The interviews are normally done by an executive coach, but can be done by the person seeking feedback. This next exercise will describe how you can gather your own information about your leadership and then analyze that information.

Leadership Self-Study

Ideal Self

Sacrifice & Renewal

Real Self

Mindful

Resonant Leadership

Learning Plan

A 360° View of You

This exercise invites you to gather insight into your strengths, behaviors, how people experience working with and relating to you, and any challenges they see you facing. Upon completion of this process, you will have a clear sense of patterns and themes that capture people's views about your strengths and challenges.

Step 1: Getting Ready

To complete the process, you need to identify up to ten people whose opinions you value and whom you believe you can interview about *yourself*. Selecting the people to talk with is a very important step.

Identify people who know you in different contexts, roles, and relationships. You want a variety of perspectives so that you can glean some lasting truths from looking across the interviews for repeating patterns. People must be willing to talk openly with you—about you. They should know you. In other words, they must have direct experience of your behaviors and routines. So don't pick the neighbor you rarely see. Choose a neighbor you've worked with on a committee or at your children's school.

The same rule applies to your work relationships. Select from a broad range of people: peers, direct reports, a close friend, a supplier, and (possibly) your boss. This last suggestion should be considered carefully—is it safe to interview your boss? Is he or she able to have this kind of conversation without feeling threatened? Will you stir up trouble if you do this? Be sure that your boss, and everyone you choose, is safe to talk with.

As you ask people to participate, be sure to let them know that the purpose of this process is for you to gain insights that will enable you to become more of the person you want to be. You are doing this because you want to change and grow. This attitude is important for people to know about, and your stance will enable them to be more frank and straightforward with you. You may feel shy to ask people to spend time focused solely on you. If you are clear about the purpose with them, 99 percent of people are more than happy to take the time to talk with you, and once you start the conversation you will both become deeply engaged. Most people truly enjoy helping others work on becoming a great leader and person. If you are open, earnest, and curious, they will be, too.

Leadership Self-Study

Step 2: The Conversations

Many of us have conducted interviews for a variety of purposes. This is not a traditional interview. Gathering data on another person is easier than getting data on yourself, so there are some special recommendations for interviewing people about yourself:

1. Be open to and objective about hearing what people have to say.
2. You risk damaging a good relationship if you respond to the interviewee in a negative way, so work on being completely nondefensive about what you hear.
3. Try to bring an attitude of curiosity and wonder to the process.

There are three goals for the conversations, and the order of priority presented here is important. The first goal is to strengthen the relationship you have with the person. The second goal is to fully hear the perspective and experience of the person you are interviewing. The third goal is to gather information about yourself that you may not be aware of, but that is important to the person you are interviewing. The purpose of this exercise is to get information that will help you, not to debate or try to adjust in *any way* people's perspectives about you.

Setting Up the Interview

Find a comfortable place away from the flow of work or family, where you will not be disturbed. Begin by establishing a connection with the person. Take the time to settle into the conversation. You may want to inquire about his or her health or family or something else of personal interest. Be sure to listen carefully (a hallmark of a resonant leader) when he or she responds. Your goal is to develop a comfortable, safe environment for the conversation. When both of you are ready, review the purpose of the conversation, stating clearly that it is confidential, that you appreciate and welcome his or her candor and willingness to help you learn and grow.

Review how the information shared with you will be used to help you develop. Prepare to take notes and let the person know why you are writing things down.

Throughout the conversation, it is critical that you do not "lead the witness" or pursue fixed ideas about yourself that you want to confirm or disconfirm. You need to be intentionally open and follow a structure that will increase the likelihood that you will discover new truths about yourself.

Leadership Self-Study

Ask pertinent questions, such as:

What do you notice and experience as you interact and work with me?

What are three things you appreciate the most about me?

What are three things you would like me to do differently to be more effective?

As he/she responds, practice active listening and probe as needed:

Why is that important?

When I do this thing you describe, how do you feel?

What is the impact on you?

What impact do you think it has on others?

Can you be more specific?

Give an example?

You need to use your social intelligence to really get into other people's experience of you as opposed to your experience of yourself. You need to listen and try to minimize your use of filters and biases as you take in their perspective. You will need to actively manage your own emotions in the moment. You must suspend disbelief, defensiveness, jumping to conclusions, filling in the blanks with your own thoughts, or becoming too enthusiastic.

Taking notes is important, because you will need to review people's responses and analyze your information. It is possible that you will hear opinions and information that will cause you to feel strong emotion—note taking will help you to stay focused. It also prevents the emotions from interfering with your recall of what was said. Take notes with the intent of providing quotes to support themes. This means you should try to capture as many comments verbatim as you can. Balance this, of course, with staying connected with the person and making eye contact.

When you are done, compliment the interviewee (on his/her creativity, openness, courage, or any other positive attribute displayed) and review the purpose of the interview and confidentiality. Express your gratitude for his or her time and insights. Invite the person to check in with you as you work to develop yourself. He or she will likely be very interested in what you decide to pay attention to, and ultimately, your interviewee may even be a good resource for you as you pursue your development.

Leadership Self-Study

Step 3: The Analysis

Since you are attempting to gain insight into your Real Self, it's important to look for breadth of perspective as well as probe for depth of insight. Each of the people you have talked with has a "real" sense of you. Your next challenge is to look across the conversations for patterns and to be open to insights that provide you with a new way of understanding how you lead and impact people.

Thematic Analysis: Deciphering the "Truth"

Thematic analysis is a research methodology that helps us to make sense of subjective information (e.g., peoples' perceptions of you); this is sometimes called qualitative information. Thematic analysis is a way of *seeing*, *a way* of *making sense* out of seemingly unrelated material, a way of *analyzing* qualitative information.[a]

Read all your interview notes. This is your data set. After you have read through the data set a few times, make notes about possible themes you see across the interviews. A theme can often be seen in patterns of people's perceptions: similarities in the words people use; recurring activities, meanings, feelings; or metaphors that people use in describing you. You may also notice important concepts, observations, or ideas that are often repeated, or emotionally charged stories or insights. You will also want to pay attention to the anomalies: rare insights that are surprising, but hint at a truth.

To home in on a few themes about yourself, you need to think systemically—what are people saying about your strengths and challenges? What patterns are there in people's collective experience of you? You need to go beyond assumptions, consider multiple hypotheses, recognize patterns, and guard against your biases.

Step 4: Prepare a Report for Yourself

The final step is to collect your themes into a report. The report will likely include five to eight major themes, and quotes that prove each theme to be true. First prepare a document with the theme headings, leaving space in between. Using different-colored highlighters, identify the quotes that jump out at you and seem to fit a theme. Cut and paste the quotes under the relevant theme heading. After you have a number of quotes to support each theme, check for internal consistency in the grouping. For the report, choose five to seven quotes that seem to best illustrate the theme.

Leadership Self-Study

Special Note: If you have a theme that is based on an anomaly or a particularly insightful part of a conversation, attempt to support the theme through a combination of quotes and your own interpretation of what people said. If you find it difficult to find enough quotes (i.e., from more than one person) to support this insight, it may not be a theme. However, if it provides useful insight to you, it should still be captured on the report.

Finally, you can take this one step further: Write a paragraph or two about each theme, including evidence to support it, what it means to you, why this is important.

You now have a qualitative assessment of your strengths and areas for development from the perspective of people you interact with. You also have a coterie of individuals who have contributed to your development. Thank them, and thoughtfully consider what you have learned from this experience.

[a]Richard E. Boyatsis, *Transforming Qualitative Information: Thematic Analysis and Code Development* (Thousand Oaks, CA: Sage Publications, 1998).

A Brief Interview

An alternative process that gives you personal information, but is not collected from as wide a variety of people, is the interview approach described in the "Walk and Talk with a Mentor . . . " exercise. Follow the same guidelines for talking about yourself as described in the "Leadership Self-Study" exercise, and choose individuals whose perspective will enrich your understanding of yourself. Mentors and mates tend to have long and deep relationships with you, while children can often speak eloquently and frankly about being in a relationship with you and looking up to you.

Walk and Talk with a Mentor . . .

Ideal
Self

Sacrifice
& Renewal

Real
Self

Mindful

Resonant
Leadership

Learning
Plan

. . . a Child and a Mate

Take a few minutes to reflect on the exercises you did in chapter 4 about your Ideal Self. Given where you want to go, what do you need to know about who you are today? What questions can you ask a mentor, a child who knows you, and your intimate partner, who knows you well?

Go for a long walk with each of these key people in your life and listen carefully as they and you discuss who you are today—your strengths, what you do well, where you stumble, your habits, and any other observations they can share. Be sure to set the tone for the inquiry by letting them know how interested you are in their opinions.

After each walk, take a few minutes to write down what they said. After you have completed your walks, review your notes and conduct a mini-thematic analysis as described in the "Leadership Self-Study" exercise.

Environmental Scanning

Another way to examine yourself is to look closely at your environment. In "Clues About Me in My Environment," you will scan your physical environment for clues about you and in "Emotional Landscape" about the emotional reality of others. Doing these exercises is also a good way to practice mindfulness by slowly and carefully observing the external world around you.

Clues About Me in My Environment

Take photographs or spend some time looking carefully at several spaces in which you live and work. Let's start with work.

Stand in the doorway of your office or other place where you work. Look around.

Is the space neat and orderly or messy? Is it comfortable and lived in or is it chaotic? Is it clean? How is the space laid out? What furniture do you have in the room? What does this say about your style and values?

What are the decorations? What do they tell us or say about what is important to you? What do you like to look at? Your space is a personal statement. What does it say about you?

Clues About Me in My Environment

Now, do the same for each room in your home or apartment. If you travel a great deal, do the same in a few of the hotels in which you stay. What do these places say about you, about what you value and what is important to you?

....

....

....

....

....

....

....

Leaders lead people, who are constantly assessing and trying to make sense of these leaders and their experiences. It is important, therefore, to stay current and attuned to the changing emotional reality of your groups, relationships, and organization, as shifts within them will deeply affect how your leadership is experienced. Resonant leaders are constantly attending to and attuning themselves to the people they lead and the contexts of this leadership. The reflective questions in "Emotional Landscape" can provide insight into your current leadership situation.

Emotional Landscape

**Exploring the Emotional Landscape
of My Leadership Environment**

This is a series of questions about the setting, tone and, atmosphere and the emotional reality that surrounds you. As you answer the questions, try to hold vivid images of your team and/or organization in mind.

What are the predominant emotions present in the environment where you lead? What are the reasons for these emotions?

....

....

....

Is your organization or team stable or in any sort of transition? Describe that in some detail.

....

....

....

What is the atmosphere of the group and organization you are leading? Think of a few words that describe the emotional tone or feeling of the environment.

....

....

....

....

Emotional Landscape

Have there been any recent events or decisions that are influencing the emotional landscape? How are you contributing to this?

....

....

....

....

How are *you*? How is the environment affecting you? How are you affecting it?

....

....

....

....

Your experiences, roles, identities, strengths, weaknesses, and ways of moving through the world are important aspects of who you are as a person. While these factors don't always determine how you think and act, they do interact to form the palette of color from which you draw as you make choices in life, engage in relationships, and lead people. This palette is unique to you and is what you currently have available to work with. It's important to fully explore and examine your current palette as you paint a picture of your life today and in the future. You may need to expand the range of color available to you to reach your Ideal Self and dreams. You may decide that the colors of your past are no longer as inspiring to you as they once were and find yourself drawn to a new set of colors or even working in a new artistic medium.

In chapter 6, you will plan for change. Using all the exercises you have done and insights you have had as you read this book, you will develop a set of learning goals, milestones, and actions that will support your aspirations for your life and your leadership. Now you are ready to plan—for the future you want. But first, here's one final exercise to consolidate your personal insights and prepare you for change.

Personal Balance Sheet

Ideal
Self

Sacrifice
& Renewal

Real
Self

Mindful

Resonant
Leadership

Learning
Plan

Like assessing the value of a business, a balance sheet is a way to summarize your personal assets and liabilities. Using *all* of the assessments and reflection you have done so far and the form that follows, you can create your Personal Balance Sheet.

My Assets	My Liabilities
My Distinctive Strengths: things I know I do well and strengths that others see in me	**My Weaknesses:** things I know I don't do well and I want to do better
My Potential Strengths: things I could do better or more often if I focused, or things I do well in some situations and could begin to apply more broadly	**Weaknesses I Want to Change**: things I know I don't do well and want to change
My Enduring Dispositions That Support Me: traits, habits, behaviors that I do not want to change and that help me to be successful	**My Enduring Dispositions That Sometimes Get in My Way**: traits, habits, behaviors that I do not want to change and that sometimes cause me to be less effective

Chapter 6

BECOMING A RESONANT LEADER

Taking Your Desires from Awareness into Action

THE PURPOSE OF THIS BOOK is to support you in becoming the best person *and* the best leader you can be. In chapter 4, you articulated your Personal Vision after doing a series of exercises to explore your aspirations and dreams. Doing this activated the Positive Emotional Attractor within your brain—the energy generated by this attractor will sustain you as you move toward your vision. Chapter 5, by offering you an opportunity to inventory various aspects of who you are currently, provided a deep reflection on your present state. Hopefully, you reached out beyond your own self-assessment and heard directly from a few people about your current strengths and challenges. Through this discovery, you might have learned how to be even more effective as a leader and to lead more directly from your values. This chapter and the next set the stage for you to now develop your plan for moving from your present situation toward your Personal Vision.

Invariably, we need to change in order to leave behind our current ways and to achieve our desired future. What do you need to learn to make this shift? What do you need to accomplish along the way? Real, lasting change occurs when we turn our desires from awareness into action. This is the power and promise of planning to learn, which you will do in this chapter. A learning plan is a very important part of the Intentional Change process. This chapter is when we move from "I should" to "I will."

Writing a plan is not difficult—knowing what you want to plan *for* is. Assuming you have reached this point in the book by reading each chapter and doing the exercises, you have overcome the biggest obstacle to having a useful and meaningful learning plan. You have developed a personal vision, and you know where you want to go. You have inventoried your personal resources, strengths, weaknesses, and relationships and developed a sense of your Real Self. With your Personal Balance Sheet and Personal Vision in hand, you now face the challenge of creating a useful and meaningful plan to attain what you want for the next era of your life. You will now create your Learning Plan.

Organizational life is littered with unfulfilled plans and aspirations never quite achieved. Why? In light of considerable thought and study, it is clear that the vast majority of development plans fail because they are tied almost exclusively to performance and are not linked to a person's dreams, goals, or life vision. In chapter 1, you did an exercise in which you remembered the people who had helped you and those who tried to give you performance feedback. More often than not, such performance-oriented feedback—and the plans developed in response—are most closely linked to what others or an organization requires of the individual. This simply doesn't work— we adults learn what we want to learn, and others' requirements of us rarely enable us to sustain a long-term change.

The process outlined in this book is designed for you to engage your own passion for change, not to fulfill someone else's expectations for you. That is what makes this approach different and worthwhile. To be meaningful, a plan must be an important agenda for you and a guide for personal exploration, not a map to get you to where others think you should go.

So, a good Learning Plan is not a performance-improvement plan. What's the difference? There are major neurological and hormonal differences in most people's response to planning to improve performance and planning to learn and reach for their dreams. The former invokes a defensive need to prove oneself, as documented in the extensive literature on performance goal orientation.[1] A *Learning Plan* is more likely to evoke openness, flexibility, hope, and the renewal response. It arouses images of experimentation, novelty, and innovation. Planning to *learn*, rather than to *perform*, frees us to focus energy on activities that are meaningful to us—we will engage in these activities without worrying about failure or disappointing someone else.

Before developing your Learning Plan, you need to consider four critical elements that will influence what your developmental process is and how you construct it: To be useful, your Learning Plan must be suited to (1) your planning style, (2) your learning style, (3) the structure of your life, and (4) the support of others—a critical element of Intentional Change.

One word before you begin: choosing to move from reflection to action and Intentional Change is a big step, requiring self-knowledge and commitment. As you reach for your dreams, you are reaching for your personal best *as a leader*. The people who depend on you in your life and at work will benefit tremendously as your capacity for resonance grows. It matters.

Planning Style

People approach the future in different ways. As Annie McKee found in her research, people use three approaches to thinking about the future: *goal-oriented*, *direction-oriented*, and *action-oriented*.[2] Some people set specific objectives and work toward them in a structured and linear fashion. This *goal-oriented* approach was used by about half of her sample. Goal-oriented planners tend to focus on very specific goals and outcomes, which are not always tied to the pursuit of a dream or fulfilling a mission. This can mean that while these people are good at setting and achieving their goals, they are often not particularly satisfied and can be in a perpetual state of seeking the next short-term objective. It is not clear whether people are goal-oriented because this style is really the most natural for them or they have this orientation because they have learned how to set goals. Goal setting, the most traditional form of planning, is diligently taught in schools and supported by performance management systems in business.

Other people (less than a third of the sample) use a *direction-oriented* approach in thinking about and planning for the future. Although they know the general path they wish to pursue, they stop short of getting too specific.[3] They have an intense sense of purpose and mission and a willingness to be flexible regarding specific goals. In terms of both their own life's desires and the world in which they live, they see the big picture. These people tend to be highly attuned to their environment and are good at spotting opportunities that they can leverage in pursuit of their dreams or a vision. They adapt easily to changes in the environment, but stay true to an overarching set of principles, values, or a vision.

Meanwhile, a surprising number of people really do not think too much about the distant future. Totaling approximately one-third of Annie's study, these *action-oriented* planners live largely in the moment, forgoing deep thoughts about the future and long-term planning. Some of these people approach planning as an extension of a series of tasks or activities, not worrying or thinking about where these steps will lead. They choose each action according to the logic of the moment and base the next decision on outcomes of recent past actions. Still others forgo thinking about the future in any form and live in an existential present. They seem to be focused on who they are rather than who they might be or what they might do.

One size does not fit all when it comes to formulating a useful plan for your future. When leadership development programs attempt to convince everyone to use the same format and propose one "best way" to think about a person's future and plans, it is not surprising that change is not sustained.

Despite the differences, each style employs a set of skills that can be helpful in the planning process. Once you are clear on which style you prefer, you might consider including skills from the other two styles as you create your Learning Plan in this chapter. For example, if you tend toward direction- or action-oriented planning, be sure that your plan includes a few specific, measurable goals. If you tend to be goal-oriented, you won't have any trouble writing specific steps in your plan. But you might want to include room for short-term, spontaneous activities. The Personal Vision exercises will help you tie your learning goals to a picture of the future that is deeply meaningful to you. And if you are action-oriented, be sure to reflect carefully on your values and noble purpose, and put in place a few goals that can support your progress. Each of the three styles has wisdom for the other; the point is to know and honor your preference and be aware of the others as you organize activities in your plan.

My Planning Style

Ideal Self

Sacrifice & Renewal

Real Self

Mindfulness

Resonant Leadership

Learning Plan

Check the appropriate response to complete each statement.

1. **When I think about my job or career, I**

   a .... Think of specific jobs I would like to have and, perhaps, a year by which I would like to have it

   b .... Think of the type of work, work style, or culture I would like to have

   c .... Think of whom I should call to talk about a new job, or look at job postings to get an idea or see what is available

2. **When I think about taking a vacation, I**

   a .... Think of a specific place, my budget, and specific dates when I could go

   b .... Think of where I would like to go or what type of experience I would like to have

   c .... Think of where I can get affordable flights and hotel rates, or which travel agent I will ask to arrange the trip

3. **When I start a project at home or work, I**

   a .... Have a clear image in my mind of what the outcome or result of the project will be and my specific completion date or time

   b .... Have an image of what the result should be or how it might fit into my work or home

   c .... Start the project and then go shopping for supplies

4. **When I want to move into a new home, I**

   a .... Find a realtor, spell out exactly what I want, and ask him or her to set up a schedule to visit six houses or apartments that meet my requirements

   b .... Spend a few weeks talking with my partner or spouse about our ideal lifestyle

   c .... Start driving around the neighborhood looking for houses for sale or apartments for rent

5. **When I am directed to improve a skill set at work, I**

   a .... Take a series of tests, identify exactly what needs to change, and find a course that exactly meets my needs

   b .... Consider whether that skill might be valuable in my life and begin a change process only if it fits with my vision of who I am

   c .... Experiment with new behaviors and see what happens

6. **When I take a day off work, I most enjoy it if I**

   a .... Have specific activities carefully orchestrated, including a dinner reservation

   b .... Engage in a set of activities related to something I am passionate about

   c .... Let the day unfold minute by minute

7. **When I want to adopt a pet, I**

   a .... Research several breeds, prioritize, select parents or where to adopt, buy all the supplies, set up my house, and then adopt

   b .... Think carefully about what kind of pet will fit into my lifestyle, and how the pet will enhance my and my family's life

   c .... Go to the pet store or Humane Society and get a pet

Total the number of checks for each letter: **a** .... **b** .... **c** ....

a	b	c
Goal-Oriented	Direction-Oriented	Action-Oriented

The type of planning orientation with the most checks gives you an indication of your preferred planning style. This should help you understand what you typically emphasize as you plan and what you may need to deliberately build in to both support your style and to broaden your approach. This will enable you to see what kind of Learning Plan is most desirable for you, and which elements of a plan you might avoid and need to add.

Attending to how you think about the future will help you craft a plan that works for you. As you build your plan, though, you should also consider *how you learn.* A big mistake that people often make when creating a Learning Plan is to include activities that do not fit their preferred approach to learning. The result: they do not engage in the activities, and the plan falls apart. People learn in different ways, relying more or less on experience, reflection, theory, and experimentation. Knowing how you learn will enable you to select learning goals and activities that fit you and your lifestyle.

Learning Style

David Kolb's Experiential Learning Theory has been a guide for many educators and other people involved in learning and development. There are over two thousand articles written about his theory, and organizations all over the world use measurements of people's preferred learning style (e.g., Learning Style Inventory, Adaptive Style Inventory, Learning Skills Profile, and Team Learning Inventory). [4]

Experiential Learning Theory maintains that people learn through two alternating processes. First, we learn by trying to *comprehend,* or grasp, aspects of an experience and trying to *apprehend,* or understand, it. Comprehension occurs when you are in the experience and noticing what is occurring, such as your feelings and those of others. This kind of comprehension links to mindfulness as described in the earlier chapters. David Kolb calls this learning *Concrete Experience.* Apprehension occurs when you build a model or theory of how something works, or use a model or framework to understand it. He calls this type of learning *Abstract Conceptualization.*

The second alternating process is the tendency either to focus internally within yourself or to focus externally outside yourself during the experience. When focusing internally, you observe what is occurring and reflect about the experience. Kolb calls this *Reflec-*

tive Observation. The alternative is focusing on how your external environment responds when you try something. This is called *Active Experimentation.*

Although we all use each of these four modes of learning, Kolb claims that we each have a preference for two, or sometimes three, of these modes. Research has shown that this preference explains which learning experiences you find exciting and which you find far less engaging. This helps you identify the ways and situations in which you learn most efficiently. If you want to discover your preferred learning style and understand how your style will help determine which actions to take as you design your Learning Plan, take the test at www.hayresourcesdirect.haygroup.com.

Resonant Relationships for Growth

An important and often ignored step in the process of Intentional Change is to enlist the support of others. Leadership is relational, and personal and professional growth is enhanced when you involve key people who rely on you and care about you. Perhaps you have a personal coach who can encourage your growth and development.[5] You may want to go back through the exercises in this book and reflect on people in your life who can support you as you work toward your learning goals. Who can provide honest feedback as you try new behaviors? Who offers emotional support? Who is excited by your potential? Who has a vested interest in your growth? The next exercise invites you to develop a list of key people who care about you and who can provide unique kinds of support.

Personal Board of Directors

Ideal Self · Sacrifice & Renewal · Real Self · Mindfulness · Resonant Leadership · Learning Plan

The objective of this exercise is to help you prepare sources of help and guidance for the next era of your life. We all need other people with whom to talk and discuss our Personal Vision, Personal Balance Sheet, and Learning Plan—and our progress on each. The people who can guide and help us on this journey should be those with whom we have a trusting and resonant relationship. They may be some of the people you used in your Leadership Self-Study. These key relationships may or may not be mutual; they could help only you, or they could help both parties in the relationship. Borrowing on an organizational concept, you can call this group of people your Personal Board of Directors.

Whom would you like to have on your Personal Board of Directors? Fill the seats with the names of people you want on your board. You may have as many as eight; try to have at least three.

Once you have developed your list, you can discuss this exercise with each of the people on the list. In other words, you should enlist them or ask them to be on your Personal Board of Directors. Once you have had that conversation, circle the name on your list or diagram.

Continuous Improvement and Refinement

The fourth discovery in Intentional Change Theory involves practicing desired changes by using life as a learning laboratory. To develop or learn new behavior, we must find ways to learn from current experiences. That is, the experimentation and practice do not always require attending courses or development programs. They may involve mindfulness—trying something different in a current setting, reflecting on what occurs, and experimenting further in a variety of settings. Taking new action in everyday life stimulates feedback from within us and from others. Continued practice in a variety of safe settings increases the likelihood that the new behavior becomes a habit. As we adopt new responses, patterns of behavior, and capabilities, we are rewiring our brain. Research shows that we can establish new neural pathways that allow us to break or reroute old responses.[6]

Experimentation and practice are most effective when they occur in situations in which you feel safe.[7] This sense of psychological safety creates an atmosphere in which you can try new behavior, perceptions, and thoughts with relatively less risk of shame, embarrassment, or the serious consequences of failure. The challenge is to practice to the point of mastery, not merely to the point of comfort.

After a period of experimentation, we usually feel more comfortable practicing new behaviors in the actual settings where we wish to use them, such as at work or at home. During this part of the process, Intentional Change begins to look like a continuous-improvement process.

Constructing Your Learning Plan

You are now ready to create a Learning Plan to guide you during the next era of your life and work. Using all the insights you have gained from the earlier sections of this book, you now need to identify what you should do and learn to get closer to your life vision.

There are infinite possibilities for what you might incorporate into your Learning Plan. You may want to learn new skills or improve an existing ability. Perhaps focusing on the key emotional and social intelligence competencies described in Chapter 2 will enable you to achieve at work and in life the kind of relationships that you wrote about in your Personal Vision. Or, for example, if you would like to run your own business someday, you may need to work on your business knowledge or technical skills such as accounting and finance. You may also need to build a strong local network among potential clients or customers, long before your business opens its doors. Or, let's say you want to work with disadvantaged children, but currently don't know much about their lives. A learning goal could be to gain a deeper understanding of their situation, psychology, and programs that have proven successful with this population of young people. The possibilities for learning goals to help you achieve your dreams are endless and exciting! There is only one cardinal rule: each learning goal must link to your Personal Vision.

My Learning Edge

To begin the process of articulating your learning goals, it helps to review all that you have learned and done so far in this book. Find a quiet place to sit, and go back through the exercises. Start by reading your Personal Vision, and then look at your Personal Balance Sheet. Read some of your notes about your past, your present, and your future.

What stands out about how your current strengths will help you move toward your Personal Vision?

....
....
....
....

Are there gaps between who you are now and who you want to be in the future or how you want to live your life?

....
....
....
....

What major changes might you need to make if you are to achieve your vision?

....
....
....
....

My Learning Edge

Identify two to five themes related to what you would like to do, be, or achieve.

....

....

....

....

....

....

....

Now it is time to turn these insights into learning goals. What do you need to learn or accomplish to begin reaching your Personal Vision? Learning goals should be big and complex. They should require time and hard work to accomplish. Your goals should not be unreachable, however, and you may want to do a reality check as you develop them. It often helps to share your initial ideas about these learning goals with another person or two—consider people on your Personal Board of Directors.

Your personal planning style will determine how you write these goals. You can express them in any way that resonates with you. The time horizon for the goals can vary, but most significant learning goals are accomplished over the long term—even as much as five to seven years. Depending on the goal, you could even take a longer view—ten to fifteen years. Of course, many people can accomplish major learning goals over a shorter time.

Again, it is essential that each learning goal relate in some way to your overall vision for your life, now and into the future. The goals should build on your strengths, as well as challenge you to overcome limitations. Consider Sopha, a woman we worked with in Cambodia as she developed a learning plan.[8] She wanted to achieve an influential position in government, where she could have a positive effect on society. Her desire was to be part of a global community of people trying to make positive differences in their countries. She knew that she would need to interact with the United Nations, the World Health Organization, the World Bank, and other global donor agencies and policy makers, and she knew that English was the common language of these agencies. Given all this, one of her learning goals was to master written and spoken English to the point that she could communicate fluently with her international colleagues and enjoy herself when she traveled abroad to international meetings.

Learning a language is certainly a big and complex goal. Thus, to achieve it, Sopha had to work hard. She had to include a variety of learning experiences, including courses, self-study, and even a short stint in a job in an English-speaking country. Maybe most importantly, this goal was directly tied to Sopha's Personal Vision, which she was passionate about. So, as you develop your Learning Plan, be sure to choose learning goals that are clearly tied to your Personal Vision and interest you. If you choose to do things you think you should do but don't care about, you are unlikely to do anything at all to reach those goals.

The Learning Plan diagram shows the relationship between your vision, learning goals, and actions, and the key relationships you will use for support.

For each learning goal you set, identify several milestones and several action steps. *Milestones* are noticeable markers that indicate your progress toward your goal. Indicate key people who can help you at any stage of the process. For example, if your learning goal is to become a senior manager in three years, a milestone might be "com-

plete the organization's advanced managerial training course." For our Cambodian colleague, a milestone was traveling to Australia for a six-month job exchange. Another leader we worked with wanted to be living a balanced life in which he was physically and emotionally fit. A milestone for him was participating in and completing a challenging triathlon.

Action steps are what you will do to reach the milestones. For instance, using the example just cited, an action step might be "register for the Iron Man Triathlon and find a running buddy to work out with." For the leader who wants to achieve an executive position, an action step could be "sign up for an eighteen-month managerial training course." Sopha cited as her action steps, "convince my supervisor to allow me to job share as I take English classes in preparation for my overseas journey" and "arrange household support for my husband and children."

Have fun with your Learning Plan. Your learning goals should reflect what you are passionate about in life. Achieving these goals will be hard work, but the payoff is well worth it. Of course, once you have completed your plan, it is time to get going! You have probably already begun to experiment with new behaviors and have changed a bit as a result of the exercises and experiences stimulated by the previous chapters in this book. Taking the time to write your Learning Plan will further ground your learning journey, and is in fact a critical step in the process. For those of you who may be direction- or action-oriented planners, writing the plan may seem redundant or unnecessary. You either know where you are going, or trust life to unfold. However true this might be, research shows that setting clear, measurable goals and actually writing them down increases the likelihood that you will reach your goals.[9]

Learning Goal 1

Ideal Self · Real Self · Sacrifice & Renewal · Mindfulness · Resonant Leadership · Learning Plan

Statement of My Learning Goal:

Milestone 1: **Milestone 2:** **Milestone 3:**

Action Steps: **Action Steps:** **Action Steps:**

Key People to Help Me:

Learning Goal 2

Statement of My Learning Goal:

Milestone 1:

Milestone 2:

Milestone 3:

Action Steps:

Action Steps:

Action Steps:

Key People to Help Me:

Learning Goal 3

Statement of My Learning Goal:

| **Milestone 1:** | **Milestone 2:** | **Milestone 3:** |

| **Action Steps:** | **Action Steps:** | **Action Steps:** |

Key People to Help Me:

Learning Goal 4

Statement of My Learning Goal:

Milestone 1:	Milestone 2:	Milestone 3:

Action Steps:	Action Steps:	Action Steps:

Key People to Help Me:

Learning Goal 5

Statement of My Learning Goal:

Milestone 1:   **Milestone 2:**   **Milestone 3:**

Action Steps: **Action Steps:**   **Action Steps:**

Key People to Help Me:

Summary of My Learning Plan

Personal Vision

Learning Goals:
1–5 Years

Milestones:
6–12 months

Action Steps:
Present to 6 months

People Who Can Help

Chapter 7

IGNITING
RESONANCE

Creating Effectiveness in Teams,
Organizations, and Communities

Y OU AND LEADERS LIKE YOU are in a position to have a significant positive impact on the people around you and the rest of
the world. So far, this book has addressed you: your aspirations, your
strengths, your challenges, and your impact on other people. Beginning with you is essential because professional leadership development cannot happen without personal growth. Now that you are at
the center of the change process, it is time to look at how you can
make positive contributions to the growth and development of the
people and groups around you.

The exercises in this book have encouraged you to find your Personal Vision and your ideal future, to gather insight about yourself,
and to formulate and begin working with a Learning Plan to take you
to the next phase of your life. The process works because it inspires
a sense of hope, excitement, and passion for personal change and

enables you to outline steps that keep you engaged and focused as you learn. In this chapter, we will share a few stories and explore the principles that work when you try to create a shared vision and bring about change in relationships, groups, and other large systems.

By definition, human systems are complicated. It is difficult to fully understand the complexity in multiperson entities and even more difficult to bring about systemic change in these entities. For simplicity's sake, we will describe change processes and exercises structured for intact teams. We will emphasize the process with leadership groups and teams because of their impact on larger collections of people. You, however, can apply the principles to any pair or group—with your spouse or partner, boss, team, organization, or community. By being true to yourself and putting the ideas and values you've rediscovered into action, you will create waves of resonance. Under your leadership, people will have countless experiences of feeling cared for, recognized, invested in, and led in ethical and resonant ways.

Resonance in a Group: It's Tangible

Vas Nair is the Chief Learning Officer at Schering-Plough, the global pharmaceutical company discussed in Chapter 2.[1] She and her team are responsible for a myriad of complex initiatives serving employees all over the world. Her highly organized team has created pristine project management processes. Team members serve their clients quickly, efficiently, and to the highest standards.

When asked about her secret for building a resonant team, Vas first praised the team's skills and project management norms. She then added that it's more than individual capabilities: "When you're asking people to give 100 percent, all the time, they have to believe they're doing something meaningful, something that matters to them.

"The leader's job is to really understand each person's sense of purpose and what binds them to the team. You need to know your people. You have to know them well enough to be able to make a connection between the team's work and overall vision and what's most important to each person on the team." Vas does this. She spends a significant amount of her time and energy on building relationships and fostering a vibrant, hopeful climate. The result: her team is not only resonant, it is also highly effective.

You know it when you are part of a group like Vas Nair's—a resonant, aligned team or organization in which everyone is seeking the same goals and excited to be on the journey together. It feels good. When this happens in families, teams, organizations, and communities, we not only feel good, we can also achieve great things.[2]

What are the qualities of such a group? Common wisdom has it that strong leadership plus a clear plan are enough to align people and mobilize their energy for action. Part of this is true: when people know where they are going, they will usually try to move in that direction. But strong leadership and even articulating a good plan are not enough to sustain momentum over time. This is why so many strategies fail. After the initial excitement, people's energy dwindles and they get distracted and fall back into old habits—patterns of behavior that may have served them in the past, but do not support a new direction.

So what does it take to build and sustain resonance in a group? There are eight Must-Dos that will support you in sparking commitment to a hopeful, inspiring future—and building and sustaining resonance with the people in your life and work.

Must-Do Number 1:
Start with Yourself

Paradoxically, if you want to lead others in building resonance and effectiveness, you must start with yourself. This doesn't mean you must be perfect or have it all figured out. It is the rare person who is totally clear, all the time, about who he or she is, where he or she is going, and why. Rarer still is the person who has reached this level of personal integrity *and* continues to learn and grow.

So, if you're not all this yet, don't worry. Most of us aren't. But the work of learning and pursuing personal growth is crucial for people who want to take resonance to the next level with a partner, a group, an organization, or a community.

Bluntly, you can't build resonance with others if you don't have it within yourself. This is important not only for you and how you feel and act, but also for the people you are leading. Humans are very sensitive to congruence between words and actions. Your followers will pay exquisite attention to whether you are embodying emotional intelligence and resonance with yourself and with them. If you ask them to look at their behavior, they will first look to see if you are "walking the talk." Naturally, if you are planning to engage your team in a process to build resonance and effectiveness, do your own work first.

Similarly, you need to get clear about your personal aspirations and how these fit into your aspirations for your group. Take a good look at yourself and how you lead the group. Be honest about your strengths and shortcomings, and begin a process of Intentional Change to bring yourself closer to your ideal. Ask for feedback.

You're off to a good start if you have reflected on and done the exercises in this book. As you prepare to work with your team, review the work you have done. And as you begin to bring others into a dialogue about resonance and effectiveness, take some time to clarify and articulate your dream for your team. Imagine what your team could be and do if you were to collectively break through some of today's barriers.

Must-Do Number 2: Build Resonance with Those Around You

Vic Gulas and Betsy Redfern of Montgomery Watson Harza (MWH Global, Inc.) are charged with building strong leadership in the top tier of their international engineering and construction firm.[3] Vic,

Senior Vice President, Chief People and Knowledge Officer, and Betsy, Vice President, Chief Learning Officer, have created a best-in-class corporate university and are viewed by executives as significantly contributing to the organization's success. An example of two people in a reporting relationship and with key interdependencies, Betsy and Vic work with the clear intention of creating and maintaining resonance in their relationship.

Both Vic and Betsy are accomplished, talented professionals. It would be easy to attribute their unit's success to their experience, good judgment, and leadership. But it really is more than that. These two people have operated from the start in a way that ensures resonance at each level. Through the resonance in their professional partnership, in their teams, and in the interactions between their team and the wider organization and between MWH and their clients, they support extraordinary engineering service to various cities and countries.

At the heart of the success is the dynamic, supportive partnership between Vic and Betsy. They have developed a shared vision of how they want to lead and what they want to model in their behavior with the team and the organizations. Despite working together for almost a decade, they take the time to explore their personal visions of how they want to work with each other and with their team in every new situation. They are constantly checking in and soliciting feedback about how they stack up to their aspirations. As Vic says, "Betsy and I are passionate about what we are doing because we know how important it is. We are collaborative. We try to marry strengths with each other and on the team. For instance, I provide strategic direction and the insight I have gained from my position as well as comic relief and safety. I am our conscience—I make sure we ask if we are focusing on the right thing."

He continues, "Betsy provides so much positive energy. She sets the environment for the team and our classes. She cares about people and leads by example. She is tenacious about task accomplishment and personal accountability, and she shows us how to care for each other and how to be a resonant team member." Betsy adds, "We have unending cordiality and a belief that anything is possible. No one can go around me to Vic without his encouraging them to take up the issue with me."

She continues, "Vic and I check in with each other constantly and are in an ongoing conversation with our team. We talk a lot and we debrief our meetings and activities a lot. This helps with alignment and knowing how we are both feeling. This extends to our team. We want people to have opinions, and we want to know what they are thinking. There is a hierarchy on the team, but we are not a leader-focused team."

Vic sums it up this way: "Our team laughs together, we celebrate everything, we instill a sense of equal voice around the table, and we call each other out when we can see that someone is feeling something. We are sensitive to each other and genuinely enjoy being together because of the climate we all help create and maintain. It really is fun. This isn't to say we don't have conflicts and issues; we do. But we are able to work through them when people really show up in this way."

The corporate university team is driven by a shared vision and a commitment to resonance. It is helping transform and improve MWH by raising the expectations of leadership and by helping three hundred key leaders tap into their passion, excel individually and as a group, and sustain resonance in their teams and beyond. It is integrating resonance and extraordinary client service into the expectations of project team behavior. Engagement has increased, managerial and leadership effectiveness is improving, and the leaders themselves report feeling renewed and energetically focused on the challenges and opportunities to make a positive difference through their leadership.

Vic and Betsy succeed partly because they work hard at establishing congruence in behavior and building resonance at each level of their human system. Individually, they are open to learning and they hold themselves accountable for modeling resonant leadership. They focus attention on their relationship—their partnership is an essential element touchstone. Having built a strong team, they enable that team to touch the organization in healthy and effective ways. Vic and Betsy are succeeding because they recognize the power of the social system and understand how each part of the system affects individuals, teams, and the entire organization.

Must-Do Number 3: Attend to All the Levels of Your Social System

A big mistake that a lot of people make is to believe that if they inspire, motivate, develop, or otherwise "fix" key individuals, the team and organization will suddenly be fully aligned and functional. This is not good enough. Creating and sustaining resonance in relationships requires paying attention to a number of powerful social realities that interact to form shared experience, norms, culture, aspirations, and emotion. Simply influencing a few individuals won't change a team or a large system very much, if at all. One person, no matter how talented or well intentioned, cannot single-handedly create and sustain resonance in a team (or an organization, for that matter). And the reverse is also true: rarely is dissonance solely the fault of one person. The problem is that many of us focus far too much on individuals and attribute success (or failure) far too much to the idiosyncratic actions of individuals.

Sadly, when we fall into the trap of believing resonance or dissonance is all about individual people, we miss the big picture. A typical example: a team is dysfunctional and dissonant. Everyone focuses attention on the disruptive behavior of one team member—talking about the person all the time, analyzing him or her at the water cooler, reinforcing one another's beliefs that this person is ruining the team. Eventually, the person gets fired and replaced. For a while, things feel better. Then, almost incredibly, the exact pattern emerges again: there is another scapegoat, the team is still ineffective and dissonant, and the same old bad habits emerge.

This familiar situation shows us that change does not happen when we focus only on individuals. Engaging the hearts and passions of the *group* is critical for creating resonant relationships, norms, and cultures that can sustain collective success over time and during times of challenge or change.[4] This is complicated. We are individuals in relationships, which form within groups, which form within organizations, which form within communities. We live in a complex social system that is fundamentally interdependent. And each level of the social system influences individual behavior.

So, resonance can rarely be sustained in isolation. One person or one pair or even one team cannot stand alone, cannot single-handedly change the emotional reality of an entire system. *Sustainable change does not happen unless several levels of the system are touched and changed in a similar manner.* The performance and atmosphere of a group are influenced by the organization to which the group belongs; the behavior and other characteristics of a couple are influenced by the couple's larger family; and a person is influenced by his or her relationships with a spouse, a boss, and so on.[5]

Understanding this interdependence and complexity is key when you are trying to shift a group or an organization toward greater resonance and effectiveness. In fact, understanding the complexity inherent in groups and organizations is rare. Rarer still is the ability to see the relationships between one or more levels of a social system. In Chapter 5, you explored your personal web of relationships. You will further explore the complexity in your own social system in the next exercise.

My Social System

Let's look at the emotional and objective reality of the systems you live in. Begin by bearing in mind the exercises you have done in this book—the sentences below will help you to reflect. Then consider four other levels of system: you and your partner, or you and your boss (dyad); you and your team; you and your organization; and you and your community.

Me

My name, nationality, age, gender, other key facts

My core values and principles

My emotional and social intelligence: strengths and challenges

What is exciting for me about my work

My aspirations for myself as a leader

My dreams for myself as a person

The key people who are in my circle of relationships

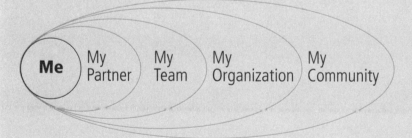

My Social System

Us: Me and My Partner or Me and My Boss

Our names and job titles

....

....

Our core shared values, and our places of difference

....

....

....

Our shared purpose, what we are trying to accomplish

....

....

....

Our strengths and challenges as a pair

....

....

....

Our joint dreams and aspirations

....

....

....

What we struggle with, our points of conflict

....

....

....

Me | **My Partner** | My Team | My Organization | My Community

My Social System

My Team and Me

Who we are: our individual names and what we call the team

....

....

Values that guide how we behave with each other

....

....

....

Our purpose as a group, what we are trying to accomplish

....

....

....

What we are proud of, what makes us feel good about ourselves

....

....

....

Our dreams and aspirations as a team

....

....

....

The challenges we face together

Me | My Partner | **My Team** | My Organization | My Community

....

....

My Social System

My Organization or Institution and Me

My organization's name and purpose

....
....

What we are funded to do

....
....

Core values that inform our work and guide our culture

....
....

Our strengths

....
....

Our dream as an organization

....
....

Our biggest challenge as an organization

....
....

Our most important stakeholders

....
....

Me | My Partner | My Team | My Organization | My Community

....
....

My Social System

My Community or Country and Me

A description of this community: who is in it, where we are located, etc.

....

....

What we have in common as a community

....

....

Our common mission

....

....

Our shared principles

....

....

Our strengths and challenges as a community

....

....

What we are most proud of

....

....

Main points of conflict and different perspectives within our community

....

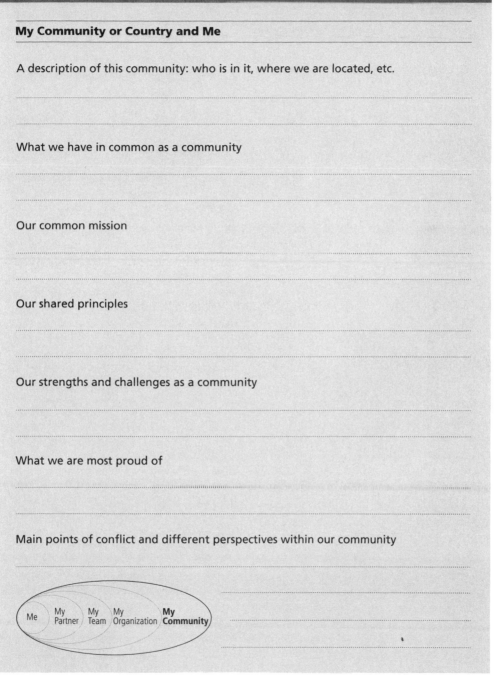

....

....

....

....

My Social System

As you answered questions about your social system, did you find areas, or levels of the system, that were easier for you to describe? What are they? What are the areas that you rarely consider unless prompted?

Can you see a pattern in how you look at levels of the system, or what you pay more attention or less attention to?

How do your values and experiences influence what aspects of social systems you pay attention to easily, and what you have to think about more deliberately?

Must-Do Number 4:
Explore the Power of Subjectivity

Some of the information you noted in "My Social System" is factual in the traditional sense—observable, measurable, and easily described. Other qualities of human systems—values, beliefs, and taboos, for example—are based on history and shared perceptions and comprise the subjective reality that people create together.

Dyads, organizations, communities, and all other groups have objective characteristics that are true *of* them. All groups also have subjective realities that are true *for* them. Ken Wilber and other students of human interaction have long argued for an expanded understanding of the complexity of social systems—one that encompasses both objective facts and subjective truths that take into account the individuals in the system and the system itself. Depending on which way you are used to looking at groups, you may miss key elements that combine to create a number of powerful truths that are part of the *system's* Real Self.[6]

Several leaders discussed in this book are successful because they pay careful and regular attention to their system's emotional reality. Dan Sontag deliberately set out to explore his company's culture and the subjective realities guiding behavior. C. J. Warner takes the temperature of her team consciously and constantly. Betsy Redfern and Vic Gulas work diligently on understanding the nuances of relationships among people and on teams.

While all these people start with themselves, they also systematically touch progressively larger systems through their leadership and practices of resonance. They listen to and work with objective organizational elements such as goals and productivity measures while also paying careful attention to subjective elements such as motivation, morale, dreams, myths, and taboos. The leaders know that this inside-out, up-and-down perspective is critical for sustainable, transformational change.[7]

But most people focus on the more objective, measurable aspects of group and organizational life. Because of the importance of values and emotions in stimulating interest and openness to change, as well as the power of authentic relationships to help sustain change, subjective reality is a particularly important area to consider in the next exercise. Here, you will get a quick picture of your group or team's subjective reality by charting it for yourself. While the exercise has been structured for the assessment of a team, you can also adapt it to assess the emotional reality of any relationship, group, or organization.

Charting My Team's Reality

Take a few minutes to consider a team that you work with. In the chart below, paint your team's emotional reality by answering a few questions in each box.

"I"—Individual

Subjective: sensations and experience	Objective: observable, measurable, behavioral
Personal values I bring to this team	My role
Norms of behavior I support	Actions I take

Charting My Team's Reality

"I"—Individual

Subjective: sensations and experience	**Objective:** observable, measurable, behavioral
What motivates me	Time I spend on these relationships
My Operating Philosophy	Outcomes that I use to measure our success

"We"—Collective

Subjective: sensations and experience	**Objective:** observable, measurable, behavioral
Explicit and implicit norms	Team structure: formal roles, responsibilities, and hierarchy
Values that drive our choices	Targets, budgets, strategies we follow

Charting My Team's Reality

"We"—Collective

Subjective: sensations and experience	Objective: observable, measurable, behavioral
Language we commonly use to describe our team	Community and country laws and policies that govern how we work
What we believe about conflict	Organizational rules, policies, and goals that govern our group's work and behavior
Emotional events that influence us	Historical events that have shaped us

It is likely that you are already thinking in some of these terms. But if you are like many people, you have been trained to pay more attention to the objective, measurable reality of an individual or a group—the information in the right-hand column of the exercise. You may also find it easier to articulate both objective and subjective realities as they relate to understanding an individual. Add this up, and you may not be fully attending to the entire spectrum of things that influence behavior and emotions in your key partnerships, teams, organization, or community.

Very often, leaders have a favorite level of the system to which they attend, habitually looking at issues from the perspective of the group, or the organization, or individuals. We need to expand our comfort in attending to multiple levels simultaneously. At the very least, it is highly likely that you and your partner, team members, or other parts of the organization or community are paying attention to different aspects of reality. This is one of the many reasons that working in and across relationships gets complicated: true emotional alignment is difficult, and even simple communication eludes us.

Must-Do Number 5: Discover Your *System's* Real Self

Many people have a preferred or habitual way of paying attention to the subjective and emotional reality of groups. And we often see this system's reality only through the lens of *our* beliefs, personal history, roles, and biases. The challenge is to expand what we notice. Nevertheless, your perspective is valid, of course, and is a good starting point.

To go beyond your habitual lens, you need to get as many perspectives as possible and to meld them into a picture that conveys a shared sense of what is really going on in the group. What are the shared principles, values, beliefs, myths, experiences, and the meaning made of them? What are the shared thoughts, feelings, and culture of the group? These are all elements of the group's emotional reality—elements that significantly affect behavior at the individual and group level.[8] For instance, a team that has consistently missed its targets may have developed a sense of hopelessness or victimization; until this emotional characteristic of the team is recognized, addressed, and changed, the team will probably continue to underachieve. A couple that has weathered life's challenges with good humor and resonance will probably have developed an emotional reality characterized by resiliency, optimism, and patience.

So how do you discover the shared emotional reality of a group? In chapter 5, we presented a rigorous process to investigate perceptions of your leadership strengths and weaknesses. We use a similar process to uncover the emotional reality, including both aspirations and challenges, of the group or system. The process itself, called *Dynamic Inquiry*, unleashes the passion and commitment people feel when they are truly listened to, given consideration, and involved in envisioning the future of the systems in which they live and work.[9]

The process involves engaging leaders and other group members in confidential conversations to describe themselves, their team, the organization, and the leadership when these elements are working at their best and when they are less effective. In the conversations, a relationship between the interviewer and interviewee is built consciously. The intent is to create trust, resonance, and an environment where people can tell the truth. This then gives the interviewer the right and permission to probe deeply and respectfully into the person's beliefs and feelings about the group or organization. Together, the pair can explore what would lead to greater effectiveness for the individual, the team, the organization, and the leadership group.

Specifically, you, the interviewer, should ask questions about what each level of the system *needs* if it is to be successful. You will need to push people beyond superficial or pat answers—"why" questions help you do this. Questions might include those directed at the person himself or herself: "What do you need in order to be effective in your job or in this organization?" This might be followed by "Why is this important to you? Tell me more about why this is so important." This basic model can be followed as you explore the other levels of a system: teams, divisions, the organization, and, possibly, top leadership. A note of caution: this method is powerful, because you are inviting people to think deeply about the underlying issues as well as the strengths in their organization. You are also asking them to consider dynamics beyond their immediate concern. You need to be sure that people trust you and that you treat what they tell you with the greatest respect.

When the interviews are complete, you need to be careful about how you look at this data. Don't get hooked by your pet peeves or seduced by the opinions that match your own. Rather, you need to conduct a thematic analysis to understand patterns and trends in the group or organization's emotional reality, including aspirations and vision of the future. The results of this analysis can be used by leaders and the participants in the interviews to begin the change that will help the organization achieve its dream.

This process supports a group, an organization, or a community to explore its collective emotional sense in the deepest way. Because of the very relational conversation that connects with and respects individuals and their experiences, and then the thematic analysis of patterns across the group experience, a shared picture of the group's Real Self emerges.

Must-Do Number 6:
Engage People's Hearts and Minds

Once you have engaged people in jointly exploring their aspirations and the emotional reality of the team, it is time to bring the team together to explore a collective vision about what the members can do together. But getting people to break old patterns of communication and to see each other holistically and as complex human beings isn't easy. To do so, you have to help people find new ways of seeing each other, yourself, and the group. Engaging the hearts *and* minds unleashes energy, facilitates effective communication, and creates interdependent commitment to a change process. Just as in an individual person, engaging the Positive Emotional Attractor in a group through articulating the ideal future is energizing and exciting. This energy helps create essential momentum for change. People have the courage and the power to collectively face almost any challenge. How can you do this? Here are a few tips:

- Take people out of their usual habitat. Get out of the office. Don't try to do this over a typical business dinner or cocktail party. That kind of social interaction is as habitual as behavior at the office—and it seldom leads to the connection that builds long-lasting resonance. Stay out of hotel conference centers, golf courses, and spas. Why? Because most people have a script for how to behave in such situations— and your job is to help people throw away the scripts and build meaningful human connection and relationships.

  Try, instead, to find a location that is really different and preferably close to nature. Maybe you will find a lodge in the mountains, some ancient ruins, or a beautiful, quiet park. Maybe you will simply go to someone's backyard. Whatever you choose, plan carefully. Make sure that you will have privacy, relative comfort, and safety. The environment shouldn't inadvertently single people out—for example, if your group has people who are not physically fit, make sure they can participate safely and without shame.

- Ahead of time, you will have selected a few discussion topics and activities that will enable people to get to know each other. Ensure that the flow of conversation moves from light and safe to more intense and just a bit risky. Set ground rules, such as respect, honesty, and confidentiality.

- Many of the exercises in this book lend themselves well to this process. If you use them, however, be sure you have thought about the flow—don't just pick your favorites. Then, ahead of time, think about how you will move people through doing the exercises (the easy part), to talking about what comes up, to coming to some conclusions about your pair relationships (with your boss or each of your subordinates), group, organization, or community.

- Even group members who have worked together for years find the experience of "meeting each other" by sharing more of themselves and their lives enlightening and even thrilling. Your first step is to help the group members get oriented and connected. One good way is to give people the chance to do, and then talk about, some of the exercises about their Ideal Self, Personal Vision, and Learning Plan.

For these tips to work, you need to bring resonance, your own sense of hope, and compassion for the team members and for the group as a whole, to your leadership. The team will open up to possibilities, and your leadership presence in this phase is critical to overcome cynicism, initiative overload, and the hopelessness that accompanies so many experiences of group life and self-serving leadership.

But how, then, do you go from personal visions to a collective picture of the future? You need to find out what is shared. It is more than likely that people's personal visions have a few commonalities—hopes for families, lifestyle, professional success, the kind of group they want to be part of, a way of working together, and so forth. Don't let this go unnoticed. When conversations about people's personal hopes are authentic and respectful, openness to share a vision grows. Like a double helix, a parallel and linked process can unfold as people consider their team's vision and connect it to their own desires and dreams.

Then, go back to what you know about your team's mission, purpose, and current challenges. Review together the outcomes of your Dynamic Inquiry. Consider your team's emotional reality in terms of whether your norms, habits, and culture will support you in attaining your vision. Or will you get in your own way? What is the strategy you are following or trying to implement? Do your patterns of interaction support this? What is your team's explicit charge? Its implicit charge? Are you all on the same page? Putting it all together—a clear picture of your team's objective reality and its emotional reality—

provides you with a comprehensive, collective vision of what your group can be and can do in the future.

Must-Do Number 7: Unleashing Resonance Through Collective Visioning

Over twelve hundred people baked in the sun as they walked along a hot, dusty path in pairs and small groups talking about their personal aspirations as leaders and the challenges they faced in the current pharmaceutical industry's climate. No one seemed to notice the heat: they were completely engaged in dialogue. When they arrived at a campground, Fred Graff, then Vice President of Sales for Sepracor, approached the microphone and got people's attention.[10]

For the next ninety minutes, this group of executives and sales leaders debated how they could create an innovative pharmaceutical company and how they should lead it. The energy unleashed was palpable. They alternated between small-group discussions and community debate, and in less that half a day, they had a full-blown plan for the culture they would create and the leadership behaviors they would use to reinforce their values and achieve their goals. By the end of the day, everyone had participated in envisioning the future, agreed with the plan, and, most importantly, was emotionally invested.

The work Fred and his team did would normally take a group days, weeks, or even months—not a mere few hours—to do. How could they come to agreement so fast? First, they had followed the "Must-Dos" outlined in this chapter. Fred had worked diligently to build his capacity for resonant leadership and to articulate his vision. He and his leadership team had passionately discussed the possibilities of creating a different sort of pharmaceutical sales culture and a truly innovative upcoming drug launch; they were committed to this vision. Over the weeks before this meeting, people had worked together in small and large groups, both deciphering their current state and building excitement around the opportunities and challenges the new organization and the product launch posed. The people had rigorously assessed the objective situation—their market and organizational structures—and had examined the emotional reality of the top team and the organization's culture through Dynamic Inquiry. Finally, at this event, they brought people together to engage in real dialogue about themselves and the future.

Sharing a Resonant Vision

We have used the following exercise with groups like the Sepracor leadership team to help people imagine the future of their organization or community. If you choose, you might use such a process with your team. Using the exercise as a guide, you can ask people to envision their noble purpose and the contribution their organization or community could make, how leadership and other important relationships are enacted, and what individual leaders' specific roles and behaviors could be to help the organization get to the desired future.

Creating a Shared Community Vision

This exercise is a way to engage a lot of people in a process of envisioning a positive future for the community or organization they belong to. The exercise involves personal reflection, small-group discussions, emotionally engaging presentations of key themes, synthesis across small groups, personal commitments, and manager-direct-report aspiration discussions. It is by no means a complete process, but a way of encouraging people to imagine the future together.

Step 1: My Dream for the Organization

Imagine you are now living ten years into the future. Close your eyes, and picture your team, organization, or community as you want it to be. Paint a picture in your mind.

What is the most exciting aspiration you have? What positive impact can you have? Consider your team, organization, or community's noble purpose—its role in the world, how leadership is enacted, the tasks you are engaged in, the ways you interact with other communities and organizations, the relevant social structures you have, how you learn, how you take care of people's well-being, the state of any particular issues that you struggle with, and so on. Note some characteristics below.

My Vision of Us in Ten Years

Who we are: ....

....

....

....

....

What we do: ....

....

....

....

....

Creating a Shared Community Vision

The values that guide us: ....
....
....
....

Our key goals and accomplishments: ....
....
....
....
....

What we are proud of: ....
....
....
....
....

Our attitude toward our customers: ....
....
....
....
....

Our attitude toward the people we lead: ....
....
....
....
....

Creating a Shared Community Vision

Our attitude toward the other groups and functions we interact with: ....

....

....

....

Our interactions with other organizations or communities: ....

....

....

....

Major changes we made to get where we are: ....

....

....

....

How we overcame the obstacles—changes implemented and the role of leadership in

the change process: ....

....

....

....

....

Creating a Shared Community Vision

Step 2: Small Groups Build the Vision

Each person presents his or her dream of the community to a small group of fellow leaders and community members as if it is happening *now*. Speak in the present tense. Ask questions of one another; respond honestly to each person's ideas. When everyone has presented, identify the points of agreement—what do you all see as a desirable outcome? What obstacles did you overcome, and how?

As you come to points of agreement and excitement and reconcile differences, craft a group point of view and presentation. You may choose to use a skit, music, poem, art, dance, or other ways to powerfully communicate your vision to the other groups. Capture the key ideas you want the audience to hear from your presentation on newsprint. Your presentation must be simple, interesting, passionate, and hopeful. You need to be clear, painting a desirable future—make people want to join you. And try to motivate *everyone*. The newsprint is your billboard of key ideas and serves as a backdrop. Putting your key ideas on the paper will enable you to avoid typical "report outs," as the critical information will be visible to all.

Step 3: Building One Vision

In a large group, each small group presents its vision of the community ten years in the future. After the presentations, engage in a community dialogue to discuss common themes, particularly exciting and creative ideas, and points of deep differences that need to be explored. Sometimes, it helps to go back and forth from the large group to small groups and back together as one. This ensures that issues can be thoroughly discussed by everyone.

Step 4: Synthesizing Commitment to Change

After deep group dialogue you may choose to have one representative of each small group caucus together to synthesize the ideas of all groups and reconcile critical points of divergence. This representative group holds the perspective and passion of each small group, and is responsible for advocating and negotiating for it. After a period of sharing, building on, weaving in, and finally agreeing on the collective vision, the representative hammers out a path toward the shared vision and a framework for implementation. The framework should include behavioral expectations at multiple levels—for individuals and for functional or thematic groups (managers, the leadership team, etc.). The representatives then return to the small groups to enroll the

Creating a Shared Community Vision

others. The representatives report back to their original small-group members (or the total community, depending on size and time available), and explain the collective path forward and the framework. Having argued for the points their small group cared about, the representatives should now be able to facilitate buy-in to the plan. Individual members should be encouraged to see that their views were synthesized into the collective vision and that if their view did not "make the cut," it nevertheless received true consideration. It is the responsibility of the representatives to ensure integrity in this process.

Step 5: Implementation
Appropriate groups (functional, regional, natural teams, etc.) hold meetings to explore how to implement the actions required to achieve the collective vision. Each person should have personal actions to take, and each group or team should have clearly articulated shared actions and agreed-upon shared accountability.

A Final Note: In the early steps of this process, it is important to adopt a Direction-Oriented approach to thinking about the future. Avoid coming to conclusions too soon, and avoid setting goals too early. In the latter steps, however, you will need to adopt a Goal-Oriented approach as you outline specific short- and medium-term goals, milestones, and actions steps.

After Sepracor created its shared vision, the company launched an organization-wide change process. For the next few months, as the organization faced the challenges of growth, a new product launch, and the integration of hundreds of new employees, the meeting in the desert served as a touchstone. The shared and vivid experience focused and stabilized this dynamic organization.

Each leader left the meeting having contributed his or her dreams for the organization to the collective aspiration for the future. The leaders also left with a personal action plan, a feeling that each member had contributed to the vision and was now more aligned with fellow leaders. They also left with a clear and shared process for engaging the Positive Emotional Attractor in their direct reports through engaging their people in personal aspiration discussions and in a positive and constructive collective journey.

To ensure that resonance would be sustained and spread throughout the organization, each manager engaged each sales representative (there were thousands) in deep discussions of the individual's personal dreams and aspirations. The resonant interpersonal connections, which occurred quite soon after the desert event, created a Positive Emotional Attractor at multiple levels—within the individuals, between the sales representatives and their managers, and across the sales organization. In this simple way, Fred Graff and his team unleashed a wave of resonance across a geographically dispersed organization, linking his larger team emotionally. This gave the participants a shared North Star that connected them and guided their decisions and behaviors. That was the subjective result of the process. Objectively, Sepracor is credited with one of the ten most successful drug launches in history.

Must-Do Number 8:
Express Personal Accountabilities
and Commitments

The process described here can be inspiring and even intoxicating. But all this is meaningless if people don't act to make the team's vision come to fruition. In other words, people need to be prepared to act on personal and collective commitments and to hold each other accountable. This sounds so obvious, but it is far easier said than done.

Again, it is the leader's job to pave the way to accountability and action. As you take your team through this process, you need to identify your specific commitments, determine what you need to change, and ask people to help you do so. What will you hold yourself accountable for? You will need to find ways to state your commitments publicly.

Then, you need to plan for others to do the same. Often, the declarations are as powerful for the team members hearing them as these statements are for the individuals making the declarations. By stating our intentions out loud in an environment of support and collective aspiration, we are signaling our willingness to contribute. This, in turn, motivates our fellow team members. It invokes a positive contagion of emotion. A caution here: sometimes people enthusiastically volunteer public commitments they may not be in a position to deliver on. It is important to carefully consider what you can authentically commit to. You have to feel it, and others need to see you follow through. The following peer-feedback exercise is one way to open up this vital exchange of commitments.

Peer Feedback and Individual Commitments

1. Form one or more small groups of up to fifteen people.

2. Each person writes his or her name at the top of a large sheet of paper. These charts are posted on the wall.

3. Then, silently, each person writes four self-sticking notes for each person: two strengths and two weaknesses, challenges, or things that need to change. Each discrete thought must be written on a separate tag.

4. Each person pastes the feedback notes on the appropriate chart for every person.

5. Then, depending on the group, you may do a silent walk-through, with time enough for everyone to read everyone's sheet. Then form a circle and have each individual voice one commitment he or she makes to the group as a result of the feedback provided. Or, with more time and for deeper exchange, have each person stand by his or her flip chart. The person then tells the group what he or she notices, and next asks for clarification of any items. Then have the individuals solicit support from the group, in very concrete ways, to help them make the changes they want to make.

The results of this exercise can then be used as input for the formulation of team member commitments. These personal commitments need to be shared, in some form, with the group, as they are important elements of the group's emerging and shifting emotional reality and are critical anchors in the collective change process.

Because so many individuals are involved in sustainable change processes, it is important to clearly address accountabilities—what are our expectations of each other? Who will be responsible for leading the different elements of the collective vision? What is the plan to take the process forward? How will energy be sustained? How will each individual continue his or her Intentional Change, and how will others know that the individual is maintaining a focus on learning?

It is essential to create structures and processes for group dialogue and public commitment about personal and collective actions and outcomes. Groups need to structure their Intentional Change by creating mutual accountability and check-in points. To strengthen this process, a group should record these conversations and commitments as they happen, creating a document to review periodically as the group measures progress.

Personal and team commitments and good intentions are only part of the picture, of course. You will most likely need to set in motion the systems and structures that support people in maintaining their changed behavior and energy. This might be as simple as reserving fifteen minutes at the end of each team meeting to ask, "How are we doing?" Or, it could be much more complex: you could change your performance management and incentive systems. Maybe you need to cascade a change throughout your organization, involve your board, or even change some of your team members.

Whatever you choose to do, it may help to remember that you are doing it in the service of achieving a vision that is meaningful to you and others. Your role as a leader can, and will, have impact; your choices about how to ensure resonance are important for all the many people who depend on you.

Businesses, schools, hospitals, communities, and even countries faced with change or crises need leaders who have resilience, hope, and the capacity to lead transformation. Certain elements are relevant in almost all situations. These elements include paying attention to the emotional reality of a group or system, using emotional and social intelligence as a foundation for leadership development, and attending to multiple levels of the human system in a change process.[11] We've taken our approach to leaders of all kinds—from plant managers to architects, teachers, CEOs, tribal chiefs, and healers. It is not easy to create and sustain resonance in one's life and with others. But leaders like you have shared with us their excitement and fulfillment as they have taken thoughtful and courageous steps toward Intentional Change and greater resonance in their lives and organizations.

You've been on a long journey of self-discovery, affirmation, and challenge. You now know how you inspire others and how you lead when at your best. You know what to do to create resonance. Answer these questions once more—drawing on all you've learned and planned for yourself.

Am I a Resonant Leader?

If you are wondering if you are a resonant leader, ask yourself these questions:

Am I inspirational? How do I inspire people?

....

....

....

Do I create an overall positive emotional tone that is characterized by hope? How?

....

....

....

Am I in touch with others? Do I really know what is in others' hearts and on their minds? How do I show this?

....

....

....

Do I regularly experience and demonstrate compassion? How?

....

....

....

Am I authentic and in tune with myself, others, and the environment? How can people see this in me?

....

....

....

Fostering Resonance in the World

We stood rooted to the ground in front of the group. We could not understand one word of what the elder was saying to us, loudly and with passion from the back of the room. As she went on for what seemed like hours, not mere minutes, her speech was increasingly peppered with a few words we did understand . . . said with obvious sarcasm and challenge . . . "Philadelphia," "America," and "Emotional Intelligence." Standing there, on the first day of our leadership program in South Africa, over one hundred participants clearly enjoyed this leader's challenge to us. There was laughter, movement, and obvious curiosity about how we would handle the situation.

This was a difficult moment. We were excited to be in South Africa, ready to share our knowledge and practices that might help people lead more effectively. We were prepared: we had begun action research projects in the country and knew, to a certain extent, what some of the issues were, both cultural and with respect to the societal issues we were hoping to impact through leadership development.

But despite our hope, commitment, and preparation, we were faced with a huge challenge. While we could not understand one word of Zulu, we did understand this leader's powerful objection. She was saying, with her words, her body, and her emotions, "Who do you think you are, and why do you think your Western, American management models have anything at all to do with what is going on in South Africa?"

She had a point.

Over the many months and years that we worked with this great Zulu woman and dozens of other brilliant South African leaders, we all learned a lot. We found common ground as we looked at resonance, relationships, and Ubuntu—the magnificent South African philosophy of group life.[19] We found that indeed, our various thoughts about leadership have much in common. Emotional intelligence, resonance, and renewal do make a difference to leadership in

South Africa. We found the same to be true in Italy, Germany, Austria, Cambodia, India, Malaysia, Brazil, Canada, the Caribbean, and, yes, Philadelphia and the United States. Practices that enhance resonant leadership translate across cultures and languages, allowing people from widely divergent backgrounds to develop their emotional intelligence, renew relationships, and sustain their effectiveness.

Leadership is a sacred act. For you and other leaders, like the woman in South Africa, to engage people's passions and dreams in the service of people and the planet is to be connected to humanity's collective past, present, and future, leaving the world just a bit better than the way you found it. As a leader, no matter what your job or role in life, you touch people. You have the capacity to create wonderful, vibrant environments that make important differences in the lives of all whom you touch. You can bring hope while also bringing results.

The best leaders *move* people. They engage people's hearts and minds and help direct people's energy, individually and collectively, toward a desired end. And resonant leaders create a climate that is ripe with enthusiasm, hope, mutual support, and commitment. In other words, they lead with emotional and social intelligence and create resonant climates that can, and do, support both leaders and followers as both groups engage in the hard work of achieving goals and bringing about change.

Back to one of our original questions: What does it take to become a resonant leader? You most likely have begun to answer that question for yourself as you have engaged in the reflections and exercises in this book. The journey takes a lifetime. We hope that you share the optimism we feel every day in this journey toward sustainable, resonant leadership.

In this book, you have traveled a great distance—from exploring your aspirations for yourself and the rest of the world, to diving into what elements combine to make you who you are, to working through how to engage the power of positive emotions in relationships, groups, organizations, and countries. These are the elements you need to create resonance within you. Hopefully, you have found places of passion, sources of renewal, and balance within yourself from which to go out and make a difference. You can transform the world by transforming yourself and by remaining energized, focused, and passionate. You can and will create ripples of resonance that will benefit the people around you and make the rest of the world a happier, healthier place.

Notes

Chapter 1

1. Resonant leadership: Resonant leaders are emotionally and socially intelligent leaders who create climates in which people can reach their potential, achieve personal and collective goals, and get results. Richard Boyatzis and Annie McKee, *Resonant Leadership: Renewing Yourself and Connecting with Others Through Mindfulness, Hope, and Compassion* (Boston: Harvard Business School Press, 2005).

2. Intentional Change: People change and develop when the future they seek is desired and relevant to their lives and work in a full and robust way. Richard Boyatzis's theory of Intentional Change has been studied over many years and with thousands of adults. See Richard Boyatzis and Kleio Akrivou, "The Ideal Self as a Driver of Change," *Journal of Management Development* 25, no. 7 (2006): 624–642; Kleio Akrivou, Richard Boyatzis, and Poppy McLeod, "The Evolving Group: Towards a Prescriptive Theory of Intentional Group Development," *Journal of Management Development* 25, no. 7 (2006): 689–709; Daniel Goleman, Richard Boyatzis, and Annie McKee, *Primal Leadership: Realizing the Power of Emotional Intelligence* (Boston: Harvard Business School Press, 2002); Boyatzis and McKee, *Resonant Leadership*; Richard Boyatzis, "Developing Emotional Intelligence," in *The Emotionally Intelligent Workplace*, ed. Cary Cherniss and Daniel Goleman (San Francisco: Jossey-Bass, 2001), 234–253; David Kolb and Richard Boyatzis, "Goal Setting and Self-Directed Behavior Change," *Human Relations* 23, no. 5 (1970): 439–457; Richard Boyatzis, "Intentional Change Theory from a Complexity Perspective," *Journal of Management Development* 25, no. 7 (2006): 607–623; and Richard Boyatzis, Annie McKee, and Daniel Goleman, "Reawakening Your Passion for Work," *Harvard Business Review*, April 2002, 87–94. From an applied perspective, we have utilized this theory in our work with individuals, teams, organizations, and networks of country leaders in development initiatives intended to facilitate clarity of direction and emotional engagement. This approach generates energy for change and enables the participants to communicate with authenticity and frankness, as well as to encourage each other's hopes. See www.teleosleaders.com for details and case studies.

3. Focusing on our strengths and dreams versus deficiencies: When we recorded reflections on "Who Helped Me? Part 1," and coded them for which aspect of the Intentional Change process was primarily involved, we discovered that 80 percent of the moments people recalled involved someone helping them extend their dreams, reach for new aspirations, or consider what it means to be a good person and to be successful. In other words, most of the memories involved people helping others to achieve their ideal selves. When we examined the moments people recalled of others trying to help them improve performance, over 50 percent of the moments involved someone giving them feedback and focusing primarily on what they needed to do to improve. That is, the focus was on their weaknesses.

The business practice of "gap analysis" is rampant as the tactic most used to help people work on a "development" or performance improvement plan. People who try to help by focusing on "data feedback" or "gap analysis" are often trying to *fix* something as opposed to trying to truly help the *person*. So, it is no wonder that many people do not change and that development can seem like a management chore. By focusing on gaps and weaknesses, we are often doing precisely the wrong thing to encourage and support change—our own or that of others. See Richard Boyatzis et al., "Coaching Can Work, but Doesn't Always," *People Management*, March 11, 2004; Richard Boyatzis et al., "Coaching for Sustainable Change," in *Handbook of Collaborative Management Research*, ed. A. B. Shani et al. (Thousand Oaks, CA: Sage Publications, 2007).

4. Positive Emotional Attractor: See Boyatzis and McKee, *Resonant Leadership*; Richard Boyatzis, "Intentional Change Theory from a Complexity Perspective," *Journal of Management Development* 25, no. 7 (2006): 607–623; Anita Howard, "Positive and Negative Emotional Attractors and Intentional Change," *Journal of Management Development* 25, no. 7 (2006): 657–670.

5. Optimism and pessimism: Martin E. P. Seligman, *Authentic Happiness: Using the New Positive Psychology to Realize Your Potential for Lasting Fulfillment* (New York: Free Press, 2002); Martin E. P. Seligman, *Learned Optimism: How to Change Your Mind and Your Life* (New York: Pocket Books, 1998).

6. Planning for the future: Annie McKee, Richard Boyatzis, and colleagues have studied how people think about the future. This research indicates that people think about the future and plan in different ways; not everyone thinks in terms of goals and action steps. Hence, it is necessary to define processes for crafting an ideal vision that takes different approaches into account. Work in this area includes Annie McKee, "Individual Differences in Planning for the Future," (PhD diss., Case Western Reserve University, 1991); Richard Boyatzis et al., "Will It Make a Difference? Assessing a Value-Based, Outcome-Oriented, Competency-Based Professional Program," in *Innovating in Professional Education: Steps on a Journey from Teaching to Learning*, ed. Richard Boyatzis, Scott Cowen, and David Kolb (San Francisco: Jossey-Bass, 1995).

7. People learn with others: M. Cecilia McMillen, Judith White, and Annie McKee, "Assessing Managerial Skills in a Social Context," *Journal of Management Education* 18, no. 2 (1994): 162–181; and Richard Boyatzis, *The Competent Manager: A Model for Effective Performance* (New York: John Wiley & Sons, 1982).

Chapter 2

1. Leadership and strategy: See Jim Collins, *Good to Great: Why Some Companies Make the Leap . . . and Others Don't* (New York: HarperCollins, 2001); Larry Bossidy,

Ram Charan, and Charles Burck, *Execution: The Discipline of Getting Things Done* (New York: Crown Business, 2002).

2. Dan Sontag: Information gathered through personal conversations and correspondence, 2006–2007.

3. Power and authority: J. P. French Jr. and B. Raven, "The Bases of Social Power," in *Studies in Social Power*, ed. Dorwin Cartwright (Ann Arbor: University of Michigan Press, 1959). In this seminal work, French and Raven outlined five forms of power (coercive, reward, legitimate, referent, and expert). This model greatly enhanced our understanding of how people perceive and use power. Many people think about leadership primarily in terms of legitimate power. In other words, we often openly recognize authority only when it has been formally acknowledged through a role or title at work, at school, in the community, or within the family. We recognize that we are expected to lead when we are head of the family, mayor, teacher, church deacon, priest, or imam. Most of us recognize the authority vested in a supervisor, manager, director, or CEO. It is easy to look at other people's titles and positions and see their power. People make the mistake of overemphasizing this type of power to the exclusion of other sources and bases, when in fact there are many forms of power. See also the seminal work by David McClelland, *Human Motivation* (Glenview, IL: Scott, Foresman & Co., 1985).

4. Emotional and social intelligence and leadership competencies: Leadership requires experience, expertise, and cognitive ability, but hundreds of studies over forty years have shown that the competenices related to emotional and social intelligence have greater impact on predicting effectiveness. See Richard E. Boyatzis, *The Competent Manager: A Model for Effective Performance.* (New York: John Wiley & Sons, 1982); Richard E. Boyatzis, "Using Tipping Points of Emotional Intelligence and Cognitive Competencies to Predict Financial Performance of Leaders," *Psicothemia* 17 (2006): 124–131; Richard E. Boyatzis and Fabio Sala, "Assessing Emotional Intelligence Competencies," in *The Measurement of Emotional Intelligence*, ed. Glenn Geher (Hauppauge, NY: Novas Science Publishers, 2004), 147–180; Daniel Goleman, *Working with Emotional Intelligence* (New York: Bantam, 1998); Daniel Goleman, *Emotional Intelligence* (New York: Bantam Books, 1995); Daniel Goleman, *Social Intelligence: The New Science of Human Relationships* (New York: Bantam Books, 2006); Daniel Goleman, Richard Boyatsis, and Annie McKee, *Primal Leadership: Realizing the Power of Emotional Intelligence* (Boston: Harvard Business School Press, 2002); David C. McClelland, "Testing for Competence Rather Than Intelligence," *American Psychologist* 28 (1973): 1–14; David C. McClelland, "Identifying Competencies with Behavioral Event Interviews," *Psychological Science* 9 (1998): 331–339; and Lyle M. Spencer and Signe M. Spencer, *Competence at Work: Models for Superior Performance* (New York: John Wiley & Sons, 1993).

5. "Know Thyself," inscribed in the forecourt of the Temple of Apollo at Delphi, is often credited to Socrates, although it actually predates him by several hundred years. The real source appears to be Thales of Milesios. See Richard Boyatzis, "Emotional Intelligence Competencies Are Wisdom in Practice," in *Handbook of Organizational Wisdom*, ed. Eric Kessler and James Bailey (Thousand Oaks, CA: Sage Publications, 2007), 223–242.

6. Presence and self-confidence: Mary Ann Rainey Tolbert and Jonno Hanafin, "Use of Self in OD Consulting: What Matters Is Presence," in *The NTL Handbook of Organization Development and Change: Principles, Practices, and Perspectives*, ed. Brenda Jones and Michael Brazzel (San Francisco: Pfeiffer, 2006), 69–82.

7. See Malcolm Gladwell, *Blink: The Power of Thinking Without Thinking* (New York: Time Warner Book Group, 2005).

8. How we learn emotional self-awareness: We have noticed that during childhood, many good leaders were close to people who helped them pay attention to and understand emotions. People who have had good emotional teachers tend to be more aware of their emotions and better able to express them in a controlled and useful way. Understanding our own emotions subsequently helps us understand others' emotions and experience empathy. Sadly, many people have not had good emotional teachers. As these people grew up, the adults around them either ignored the youngsters' emotions or told them the emotions were wrong ("you don't dislike your brother, you love him"). Many people, in many cultures, are simply not allowed to express certain emotions ("don't cry" or "don't be sad"). This is often more true for men than women. And, all over the world, circumstances such as mental illness or family violence make expressing emotions dangerous. In these circumstances, keeping a low profile is an adaptive and lifesaving response. We do see one notable exception to this rule: some people who have grown up in households affected by mental illness, abuse, or alcoholism develop extremely good emotional radar, especially with respect to negative emotions. Because survival depended on their ability to read the emotional environment and predict what might happen, these people learned early on to tune in to their own feelings and act quickly. In our experience, a surprising number of excellent leaders fit into this group. See Alice Miller, *Drama of the Gifted Child* (New York: Basic Books, 1997); Fred Branfman, "The Neuropsychology of the Playground," June 24, 2003, http://dir.salon.com/story/mwt/feature/2003/06/24/siegel/index.html.

9. Mindfulness: Ellen Langer's work on mindfulness has been instrumental in helping us understand how we human beings make sense of our world and our place in it. See Ellen Langer, *The Power of Mindful Learning* (Reading, MA: Perseus Books, 1997); Ellen Langer, *Mindfulness* (Cambridge, MA: Perseus Publishing, 1989); and Boyatzis and McKee, *Resonant Leadership*.

10. Ongoing research by us and our colleagues at the Hay Group supports the very interesting discussions of the importance of self-awareness and its role in supporting empathy a critical component of social intelligence; see Daniel Goleman, *Social Intelligence.*

11. Morgan McCall, Michael Lombardo Jr., and Ann Morrison, *The Lessons of Experience: How Successful Executives Develop on the Job* (Lexington, MA: Lexington Books, 1988).

12. Emotional contagion: People catch emotions from each other, in particular from people they pay a lot of attention to, such as parents, partners, or bosses. See a description of the research in Thomas Lewis, Fari Amini, and Richard Lannon, *A General Theory of Love* (New York: Random House, 2000). Also see Richard Petty, Leandre Fabriger, and Duane Wegener, "Emotional Factors in Attitudes and Persuasion," in *Handbook of Affective Sciences*, ed. Richard J. Davidson, Klaus R. Sherer, and H. Hill Goldsmith (New York: Oxford University Press, 2003), 752–772; and Elaine Hatfield, John Cacioppo, and Richard Rapson, *Emotional Contagion* (New York: Cambridge University Press, 1994). A particularly promising field of research is focusing on what are commonly called mirror neurons. These structures in the brain appear to be related to people's ability to notice and adapt to the emotions of others; see Charles Daney, *Mirror Neurons,* http://scienceandreason.blogspot.com/2006/02/mirror-neurons.html, February 6, 2006 [original source: "Cells That Read Minds," *New York Times*, January 10, 2006].

13. In her studies, Nadia Wager and her colleagues examined the effects of supervisors who were perceived favorably and those who were perceived unfavorably. She measured various physical responses, including blood pressure. Employees who worked under the negatively perceived supervisors showed markedly higher blood pressure as well as others signs of distress. Nadia Wager, George Fieldman, and Trevor Hussey, "The Effect on Ambulatory Blood Pressure of Working Under Favorably and Unfavorably Perceived Supervisors," *Occupational Environmental Medicine* 60 (2003): 468–474. See also Daniel Goleman, *Destructive Emotions: How Can We Overcome Them? A Scientific Dialogue with the Dalai Lama* (New York: Bantam Books, 2003), for a review of the effects of negative emotions on physical and psychological functioning.

14. Positive emotions and performance: See Barbara Fredrickson and Christine Branigan, "Positive Emotions Broaden the Scope of Attention and Thought-Action Repertoires," *Cognition and Emotion* 19, no. 3 (2005): 313–332; Barbara Fredrickson, "Positive Emotions in Organizational Settings," in *Positive Organizational Scholarship*, ed. Kim Cameron, Jane Dutton, and Robert Quinn (San Francisco: Berrett-Koehler, 2003); Goleman, *Destructive Emotions*.

15. Fred Hassan: Information gathered through personal conversations and correspondence, 2006–2007.

16. Information provided by Soni Basi, Director of Global Learning & Development at Schering-Plough. Data complied and analyzed by International Survey Research, now Towers Perrin-ISR, world headquarters in Chicago. According to Towers Perrin-ISR analysts, Schering-Plough surpassed ISR's highest standards and indeed the highest standards in the survey field, in scores on the Global High-Performing Companies benchmark, in most survey categories. What was most remarkable to the researchers, though, was the unprecedented speed of their change.

17. Positive benefits of hope and compassion, See Jerome Groopman, *The Anatomy of Hope: How People Prevail in the Face of Illness* (New York: Random House, 2004); C. R. Snyder, Kevin L. Rand, and David R. Sigmon, "Hope Theory: A Member of Positive Psychology Family, in *Handbook of Positive Psychology*, ed. Charles Richard Snyder and Shane J. Lopez (New York: Oxford University Press, 2002), 257–276. For compassion research, see Richard J. Davidson, "Toward a Biology of Positive Affect and Compassion," in *Visions of Compassion: Western Scientists and Tibetan Buddhists Examine Human Nature*, ed. Richard J. Davidson and Anne Harrington (New York: Oxford University Press, 2002), 107–130. For a discussion of left versus right prefrontal cortex activation through mindfulness and compassion, see Daniel Goleman, *Destructive Emotions*. For information on how to manage sacrifice and renewal, see Richard Boyatsis and Annie McKee, *Resonant Leadership: Renewing Yourself and Connecting with Others Through Mindfulness, Hope, and Compassion* (Boston: Harvard Business School Press, 2005).

18. Benefits of positive emotions and resonance: In recent years, the fields of affective science and positive psychology have added much to our understanding of how emotions affect cognition and individual and group behavior and performance. When people are positively challenged, hopeful, and enthusiastic, for example, they tend to be more open, adaptable, and creative; they can process more information, and can do so faster. Joseph Forgas, "Affective Influences on Attitudes and Judgments," in *Handbook of Affective Sciences*, ed. Richard J. Davidson, Klaus R. Scherer, and H. Hill Goldsmith (New York: Oxford University Press, 2003), 596–618; Alice M. Isen, "A Role for Neuropsychology in Understanding and Facilitating Influence of Positive Affect on Social Behavior and Cognitive Processes," in *Handbook of Positive Psychology*, ed. C. R.

Snyder and Shane J. Lopez (New York: Oxford University Press, 2002); Mihaly Csikszent-mihalyi, *Finding Flow: The Psychology of Engagement with Everyday Life* (New York: Basic Books, 1997). Carol Frenier, *Business and the Feminine Principle: The Untapped Resource* (Newton, MA: Butterworth-Heineman, 1997), writes: "You feel the presence of the sacred, you sense that everyone shares this feeling . . . and that your ability to communicate seems broader . . . it is astounding how much creativity comes forth in this setting."

Chapter 3

1. Mindfulness and wake-up calls: Ellen Langer, *The Power of Mindful Learning* (Reading, MA: Perseus Books, 1997); Ellen Langer, *Mindfulness* (Cambridge, MA: Perseus Publishing, 1989); Richard Boyatzis and Annie McKee, *Resonant Leadership: Renewing Yourself and Connecting with Others Through Mindfulness, Hope, and Compassion* (Boston: Harvard Business School Press, 2005). For an exploration of how wake-up calls and life's other epiphanies can help us stay on the right course, see Richard Boyatzis, Annie McKee, and Daniel Goleman, "Reawakening Your Passion for Work," *Harvard Business Review*, April 2002, 87–94. Most people, especially leaders or others who have significant responsibility, occasionally go through periods of discontent, restlessness, and possibly rejuvenation. Our research and experience unearthed some clues that indicate that we need personal or professional change, or both, to continue to be effective or happy in life and work. These clues that this is necessary tend to be a rumbling sense of unease or a sudden enlightenment when we experience a traumatic event such as a death, divorce, or major failure, or even a positive event such as the birth of a child. Once awakened, we have several strategies for managing the process of reflection and change. The strategies include calling a time-out; enrolling in a new and challenging educational program; creating what we call reflective structures (e.g., meditation, keeping a journal, prayer); working with a coach; and reframing how we are engaging in the various roles in our lives, rethinking how best to enact those roles, and consciously beginning to practice new ways of being.

2. C. J. Warner: Information gathered through personal conversations and correspondence, 2006–2007.

3. Medicine Wheel: See C. Clinton Sidle, *The Leadership Wheel: Five Steps for Achieving Individual and Organizational Greatness* (New York: Palgrave MacMillan, 2005); see also Angeles Arrien, *The Four-Fold Way: Walking the Paths of the Warrior, Teacher, Healer, and Visionary* (New York: HarperCollins, 1993).

4. Matt Doherty: Information gathered from personal conversations and correspondence, 2003–2007. See also Brad Townsend, "Adversity Only Fuels Doherty's Tenacity: SMU Basketball Coach Used Time After UNC Job to Grow as a Leader," *Dallas Morning News*, October, 15, 2006, available at www.dallasnews.com.

5. Defensive routines: Chris Argyris, *Strategy, Change and Defensive Routines* (Boston: Pitman Publishing, 1985).

Chapter 4

1. "James": We have used a pseudonym to protect this person's identity.

2. Positive emotion and efficacy: Daniel Goleman, *Destructive Emotions: How Can We Overcome Them? A Conversation with the Dalai Lama* (New York: Bantam Dell,

2003); Richard Boyatzis and Kleio Akrivou, "The Ideal Self As a Driver of Change," *Journal of Management Development* 25, no. 7 (2006): 624–642; Martin E. P. Seligman, *Authentic Happiness: Using the New Positive Psychology to Realize Your Potential for Lasting Fulfillment* (New York: Free Press, 2002).

3. Positive Emotional Attractor: Kleio Akrivou, Richard Boyatzis, and Poppy McLeod, "The Evolving Group: Towards a Prescriptive Theory of Intentional Group Development," *Journal of Management Development* 25, no. 7 (2006): 689–709. Also see Barbara Fredrickson and Christine Branigan, "Positive Emotions Broaden the Scope of Attention and Thought-Action Repertoires," *Cognition and Emotion* 19, no. 3 (2005): 313–332; Barbara Fredrickson, "Positive Emotions in Organizational Settings," in *Positive Organizational Scholarship*, ed. Kim Cameron, Jane Dutton, and Robert Quinn (San Francisco: Berrett-Koehler, 2003); Richard J. Davidson, "Toward a Biology of Positive Affect and Compassion," in *Visions of Compassion: Western Scientists and Tibetan Buddhists Examine Human Nature*, ed. Richard J. Davidson and Anne Harrington (New York: Oxford University Press, 2002), 107–130. For a discussion of left versus right prefrontal cortex activation through mindfulness and compassion, see Daniel Goleman, *Destructive Emotions*.

4. Engaging Positive Emotional Attractor to counter stress: Richard Boyatzis and Annie McKee, *Resonant Leadership: Renewing Yourself and Connecting with Others Through Mindfulness, Hope, and Compassion* (Boston: Harvard Business School Press, 2005): 154–157; Martin E. P. Seligman and Mihaly Csikszentmihalyi, "Positive Psychology: An Introduction," *American Psychologist* 55 (2000): 5–14.

5. Mental rehearsal: As mentioned in Daniel Goleman, Richard Boyatzis, and Annie McKee, *Primal Leadership: Realizing the Power of Emotional Intelligence* (Boston: Harvard Business School Press, 2002), Laura Wilkinson won the ten-meter platform diving Gold Medal in Sydney with a taped foot. She had broken it just months before the Olympics, and she attributed her win to the visualization that her coach made her do. As her ankle healed, she sat by the pool for up to six hours a day, mentally watching herself walk to the ladder, climb it, get set for the dive, dive, enter the water, swim to the edge of the pool, get out and do it again, and again and again. See also Jim Loehr and Tony Schwartz, "The Making of the Corporate Athlete," *Harvard Business Review*, January 2001, 120–128; I. Meister et al., "Playing the Piano in the Mind: An fMRI Study on Music Imagery and Performance in Pianists," *Cognitive Brain Research* 19, no. 3 (2004): 219–228.

6. Visual imaging prepares the brain for action: Gabriel Kreiman, Christof Koch, and Itshak Fried, "Imagery Neurons in the Human Brain," *Nature* 408 (2000): 357–361. On how using neural connections over and over strengthens them, see G. Edelman, *Neural Darwinism: The Theory of Neuronal Group Selection* (New York: Basic Books, 1987), 58; Cameron Carter et al., "How the Brain Gets Ready to Perform," presentation at the 30th Annual Meeting of the Society of Neuroscience (New Orleans, November 2000); Tara Bennett-Goleman, *Emotional Alchemy: How the Mind Can Heal the Heart* (New York: Harmony Books, 2001).

7. Richard Boyatzis, "Intentional Change Theory from a Complexity Perspective," *Journal of Management Development* 25, no. 7 (2006): 607–623; Anita Howard, "Positive and Negative Emotional Attractors and Intentional Change," *Journal of Management Development* 25, no. 7 (2006): 657–670; Boyatzis and Akrivou, "Ideal Self as a Driver of Change."

8. Noble purpose and the effect of reflection and contemplation on our dreams and effectiveness: A number of scholars and practitioners are reviving interest in

how our calling, purpose, or moral stance affects how we envision our individual and collective future and our effectiveness. See Josh Freedman, *At the Heart of Leadership: How to Get Results with Emotional Intelligence* (San Mateo, CA: Six Seconds, 2007); Doug Lennick and Fred Kiel, *Moral Intelligence: Enhancing Business Performance and Leadership Success* (Upper Saddle River, NJ: Pearson Education [Wharton School Publishing], 2005).

9. Dr. Martin Luther King Jr.'s "I Have a Dream" speech is copyrighted by the King estate and Writer's House.

10. Optimism: For a review of the effect of optimism and positive outlook on leadership behavior, see Boyatzis and McKee, *Resonant Leadership*, 164–165; Seligman, *Authentic Happiness*.

11. Values clarification: These exercises are adapted from numerous instruments used to assess one's values and are based on the ideas of Milton Rokeach (*Understanding Human Values* [New York: Free Press, 1979]); and Sidney B. Simon, Leland W. Howe, and Howard Kirschenbaum (*Values Clarification* [New York: Grand Central Publishing, 1995]).

Chapter 5

1. "Jill Hu": We have used a pseudonym to protect this person's identity.

2. Daniel Goleman, Richard Boyatzis, and Annie McKee, *Primal Leadership: Realizing the Power of Emotional Intelligence* (Boston: Harvard Business School Press, 2002). See also Gordon Wheeler, *Gestalt Reconsidered* (New York: Gestalt Institute of Cleveland Press, 1991), for a thorough review of Gestalt theory and the importance of paying attention and noticing distinctive patterns of human interaction.

3. Defensive routines and resistance: See Wheeler, *Gestalt Reconsidered*, for a thoughtful consideration of functional and dysfunctional patterns of interacting with our environment and the relationships within it. See also Chris Argyris, *Strategy, Change and Defensive Routines* (Boston: Pitman Publishing, 1985).

4. This inventory is distributed worldwide by Hay Group; see www.haygroup.com for more information.

Chapter 6

1. David Kolb and Richard Boyatzis, "Goal Setting and Self-Directed Behavior Change," *Human Relations* 23, no. 5 (1970): 439–457; Edwin Locke, "Toward a Theory of Task Performance and Incentives," *Organizational Behavior and Human Performance* 3 (1968): 281–291; Joan Hollenbeck and Howard Klein, "Goal Commitment and the Goal Setting Process: Problems, Prospects, and Proposals for Future Research," *Journal of Applied Psychology* 40 (1987): 212–220.

2. Annie McKee, *Individual Differences in Planning for the Future* (PhD diss., Case Western Reserve University, 1991).

3. Different approaches to planning: The one-size-fits-all approach to planning lacked a credible alternative until Michael McCaskey suggested that some people plan by "domain and direction setting." Michael McCaskey, "A Contingency Approach to Planning: Planning with Goals and Planning without Goals," *Academy of Management Journal* 17, no. 2 (1974): 281–291.

4. David Kolb, *Experiential Learning: Experience As the Source of Learning and Development* (Upper Saddle River, NJ: Prentice Hall, 1983).

5. Coaching has been shown to be an effective way to enhance leadership performance. Richard Boyatzis, Melvin Smith, and Nancy Blaize, "Developing Sustainable Leaders Through Coaching and Compassion," *Academy of Management Journal on Learning and Education* 5, no. 1 (2006): 8–24.

6. Process of neurogenesis; stem cells and the hippocampus: Peter S. Erikson et al., "Neurogenesis in the Adult Human Hippocampus," *Nature Medicine* 4 (1998): 1313–1317; Stephan Harzsch et al., "From Embryo to Adult: Persistent Neurogenesis and Apoptotic Death Shape the Lobster Deutocerebrum," *Journal of Neuroscience* 19, no. 9 (1999): 3472–3485; Daniel Goleman, Richard Boyatzis, and Annie McKee, *Primal Leadership: Realizing the Power of Emotional Intelligence* (Boston: Harvard Business School Press, 2002).

7. Kolb and Boyatzis, "Goal-Setting and Self-Directed Behavior Change."

8. "Sopha" is a pseudonym, used here to protect this person's identity, as her Learning Plan is a personal document.

9. Goal setting and writing a learning plan increases the likelihood of goal attainment: See Kolb and Boyatzis, "Goal-Setting and Self-Directed Behavior Change," for references on goal setting. See J. Matthew Beaubien and Stephanie Payne, "Individual Goal Orientation as a Predictor of Job and Academic Performance: A Metanalytic Review and Integration," paper presented at the meeting of the Society for Industrial and Organizational Psychology, Atlanta, April 1999; David Leonard, "The Impact of Learning Goals on Self-Directed Change in Education and Management Development" (PhD diss., Case Western Reserve University, 1996), for a study of the impact of writing a Learning Plan on goal attainment.

Chapter 7

1. Vas Nair: Information gathered through personal conversations and correspondence, 2006–2007.

2. Positive groups help positive change: Jin Nam Choi, Richard H. Price, and Amiram D. Vinokur, "How Context Works in Groups: The Influence of Group Processes on Individual Coping Outcomes" (unpublished paper, University of Michigan, Institute for Social Research, Ann Arbor, 1999); Richard R. Carkhuff, *Helping and Human Relations: A Primer for Lay and Professional Helpers*, vol. 1, *Selection and Training*, and vol. 2, *Practice and Research* (New York: Holt, Rinehart and Winston, 1969); Kleio Akrivou, Richard Boyatzis, and Poppy McLeod, "The Evolving Group: Towards a Prescriptive Theory of Intentional Group Development," *Journal of Management Development* 25, no. 7 (2006): 689–709. For perspective on coaching relationships, see Richard Boyatzis et al., "Coaching Can Work, but Doesn't Always," *People Management,* March 11, 2004; Richard Boyatzis et al., "Coaching for Sustainable Change," in *Handbook of Collaborative Management Research*, ed. A. B. Shani et al. (Thousand Oaks: Sage Publications, 2007).

3. Vic Gulas and Betsy Redfern: Information gathered through personal conversations and correspondence, 2006–2007.

4. Daniel Goleman, Richard Boyatzis, and Annie McKee, *Primal Leadership: Realizing the Power of Emotional Intelligence* (Boston: Harvard Business School Press, 2002); Richard Boyatzis and Annie McKee, *Resonant Leadership: Renewing Yourself and*

Connecting with Others Through Mindfulness, Hope, and Compassion (Boston: Harvard Business School Press, 2005): 154–157.

5. There are rich and well-researched theories of how systems interact with and influence individual behavior. For a group development perspective, see Susan Wheelan, *Group Processes: A Developmental Perspective*, 2nd ed. (Boston: Allyn and Bacon, 2005). For an organizational development view, see Edgar Schein, *Organizational Psychology*, 3rd ed. (Englewood Cliffs, NJ: Prentice Hall, 1980); Edwin Nevis, *Organizational Consulting: A Gestalt Approach* (New York: Gardner Press/Gestalt Institute of Cleveland Press, 1987). For an ecological systems model that explores the impact of systems on individuals and dyads in particular, see Sonia Nevis and Joseph Zinker, "How Gestalt Therapy Views Couples, Families, and the Process of Their Psychotherapy," working paper, Center for the Study of Intimate Systems, Gestalt Institute of Cleveland, 1981; Barbara Okun, *Effective Helping: Interviewing and Counseling Techniques*, 6th ed. (Pacific Grove, CA: Wadsworth Publishing, 2002).

6. Ken Wilber, *A Brief History of Everything*, 2nd ed. (Boston: Shambhala Publishing, 2007). Wilber's four-quadrant theory follows the intellectual tradition of Descartes, Martin Buber, and Jürgen Habermas.

7. See Gordon Wheeler, *Gestalt Reconsidered* (New York: Gardner Press/Gestalt Institute of Cleveland Press, 1991); Edwin Nevis, *Organizational Consulting: A Gestalt Approach* (New York: Gardner Press/Gestalt Institute of Cleveland Press, 1987), for careful analyses of the impact of common "ground" created in systems and the impact of subjective realities that are shared.

8. Wheeler, *Gestalt Reconsidered*, 103.

9. Fred Graff: Information gathered through personal conversations and correspondence, 2006–2007.

10. Ubuntu: This philosophy or ethic focuses on people's relationships with one another and with the collective group. The word is thought to be derived from the Banta languages of Southern Africa. As a traditional concept and guiding force in many tribes, it has a profound effect on how people relate to each other and to their groups. One translation, "I am because we are," indicates that the individual lives only in relation to the group. Barbara Nussbaum, "African Culture and Ubuntu: Reflections of a South African in America," *World Business Academy* 17, no. 1 (2003).

11. Annie McKee [London] and Cecilia McMillen, "Discovering Social Issues: Organizational Development in a Multicultural Community," *Journal of Applied Behavioral Sciences* 28, no. 3 (1992): 445–460; Annie McKee and Frances Johnston, "The Impact and Opportunity of Emotion in Organizational Development" in *The NTL Handbook of Organization Development and Change: Principles, Practices, and Perspectives*, ed. Brenda Jones and Michael Brazzel (San Francisco: Pfeiffer, 2006).

12. Goleman, Boyatzis, and McKee, *Primal Leadership*. See also Cary Cherniss and Mitch Adler, *Promoting Emotional and Social Intelligence in Organizations: Make Training in Emotional and Social Intelligence Effective* (Washington, DC: American Society of Training and Development, 2000). See also Nicholas Rashford and David Coghlan, *The Dynamics of Organizational Levels* (Reading, MA: Addison Wesley, 1993).

List of Exercises

Who Helped Me?   4–5
Who Do You Lead?   15–16
Start with Your Beliefs   18–20
The Best and Worst Leaders   22–23
Name Those Feelings   27–28
Am I a Resonant Leader?   42, 210
Taking Stock   48–49
Mindfulness Check-In   50–51
Seeking Balance   53
Mindful Change   54
The Sacrifice Syndrome   58
My Defensive Routines   60–62
Wake-Up Calls   64–66
My Noble Purpose   74–76
27 Things I Want to Do Before I Die   78
The Lottery: If I Could, I Would…   79
My Ideal Life   80
My Life in the Year 20__   81
My Fantasy Job   82–83
My Dreams   84
Major Themes in My Dreams   85
My Legacy   86
My Passion   87
My Calling   88

What Will People Say About Me?   89

My Values   90–91

Philosophical Orientation Questionnaire   94–103

Circles of Life   104

My Personal Vision   106–107

Pictures of Me   113

My Lifeline   114–115

Rhythms of My Career   116–118

Transitions in Life and at Work   119

My Social Identities and Roles   122–124

My Social Web   126–130

A Letter from My Heart   131

Strengths I See in Myself   132–134

Strengths Others See in Me   134–135

Activities and Situations I Tend to Avoid   136–137

Leadership Self-Study   139–143

Walk and Talk with a Mentor   144

Clues About Me in My Environment   145–146

Emotional Landscape   147–148

Personal Balance Sheet   150

My Planning Style   156–157

Personal Board of Directors   160

My Learning Edge   163–164

Learning Goal 1   168

Learning Goal 2   169

Learning Goal 3   170

Learning Goal 4   171

Learning Goal 5   172

Summary of My Learning Plan   173

My Social System   183–188

Charting My Team's Reality   190–192

Creating a Shared Community Vision   200–204

Peer Feedback and Individual Commitments   207

Index

Abstract Conceptualization, 158
action-oriented planning style, 154
Active Experimentation, 159

Boyatzis, Richard, 138

calling, 88
Cheeley, Ron, 34
collective visioning, 198–205
compassion and leadership, 39
Concrete Experience, 158

defensive routines, 59–63
direction-oriented planning style, 154
Doherty, Matt, 55–58
Dynamic Inquiry, 194

ego defense mechanisms, 137–138
Emotional and Social Competency
    Inventory (ESCI), 138
emotional intelligence, 25, 26–29
eulogy description, 89
Experiential Learning Theory, 158

fantasy job description, 82–83
future life description, 81

goal-oriented planning style, 154
Goleman, Daniel, 138
Graff, Fred, 198
Gulas, Vic, 178–181, 189

Hassan, Fred, 32–36
hope and leadership, 38–39
Hu, Jill, 109–111

ideal life description, 80
Ideal Self, 9
    engaging your dreams/fantasies,
        78–85
    finding your passion, 69–71
    learning plan and, 166
    living values, 104
    passion, calling, purpose, legacy,
        86–89
    personal vision, 69–76, 105, 166
    philosophy/philosophical
        orientation, 92–103
    positive emotional attractors and,
        72
    understanding your own, 72–73
    values and philosophy, 89–92
Intentional Change Theory, 2, 8–10

Kolb, David, 158

leadership. *See* resonant leadership
Learning Plan
    continuous improvement and
      refinement, 161
    learning goals, 164–167
    Learning Plan construction, 161–173
    Learning Plan description and
      elements, 152–153
    learning style, 158–159
    personal board of directors, 160
    planning styles, 153–157
    process of learning resonance, 7–8
legacy description, 86
lottery fantasy, 79

mindfulness
    awareness of yourself, 47–51
    emotional intelligence and, 26–29
    example of, 45–47
    recognizing emotion, 29–30
    seeking balance and, 52–55
    stress and sacrifice and (*see* Sacrifice
      Syndrome)

Nair, Vas, 176–177

operating philosophy, 93

passion description, 87
personal accountabilities and
    commitments, 205–209
personal power, 14–17
personal vision. *See* Ideal Self
planning style, 153–157
Positive Emotional Attractor, 6, 72
power stress
    felt by leaders, 36–37
    Sacrifice Syndrome and, 59–63

Real Self, 9
    avoided activities analysis, 136–137
    environmental scanning, 145–148

example of appreciating, 109–111
leadership self-study, 137–143
life reflection, 112–119, 144
personal balance sheet, 150
social identity and roles and, 120–124
social world description, 125–131
strengths and gaps review, 132–135
of a system, 193–195
Redfern, Betsy, 178–181, 189
Reflective Observation, 159
renewal cycle
    defensive routines identification,
      60–63
    elements of, 38–39
    mindfulness and, 52–55
    practices to stop Sacrifice Syndrome,
      37–38, 41
    wake-up calls, 63–67
resonant leadership
    beliefs about leadership, 17–21
    best and worst leaders list, 21–23
    best qualities of leadership, 20
    characteristics of a great leader,
      13–14
    described, 1–3, 42–43
    emotion's place in leadership, 29–30,
      31–32
    examining your own resonance,
      177–178
    example of, 32–36
    fostering resonance, 211–213
    help from others, reflecting on, 4–7
    how to lead example, 11–13
    intentional change and, 8–10
    leadership learning process, 7–8
    leader's resilience and, 36–39
    need for more than smarts, 25–30
    personal power analysis, 14–17
    plan for achieving (*see* Learning
      Plan)
    reactions to types of help, 6
    resonance versus dissonance, 39–41
    resonant leadership concept, 1–3,
      42–43
    rules for resonance, 33–36
    self-appraisal, 210
    teams and (*see* social systems)

Sacrifice Syndrome
  defensive routines identification,
     60–63
  example of, 55–57
  power stress and, 59–63
  prevention for leaders, 37–39, 41
  self-awareness of, 58
  wake-up calls, 63–67
self-awareness and leadership, 26–30,
  58
social identity and roles and real self,
  120–124
social intelligence, 25–26
social systems
  attending to all levels of, 181–182
  building group resonance, 178–181
  collective visioning, 198–205
  complexity of, 182–188
  engaging hearts and minds, 195–198
  examining your own resonance,
     177–178
  leadership example, 176–177

  personal accountabilities and
     commitments, 205–209
  qualities of a resonant group, 177
  subjectivity and, 189–193
  system's real self, 193–195
social world description and real self,
  125–130
Sontag, Dan, 11–14, 189
subjective reality in social systems,
  189–193

teams and resonant leadership. *See*
  social systems

vision, personal. *See* Ideal Self

wake-up calls, 63–67
Warner, C. J., 45–47, 189
Wilber, Ken, 189

About the Authors

Annie McKee is a cofounder of the Teleos Leadership Institute and adjunct professor at the University of Pennsylvania Graduate School of Education.

Richard E. Boyatzis is a professor in the departments of Organizational Behavior and Psychology at Case Western Reserve University. He is also visiting professor of Human Resources at ESADE in Barcelona.

Frances Johnston is a cofounder of the Teleos Leadership Institute.

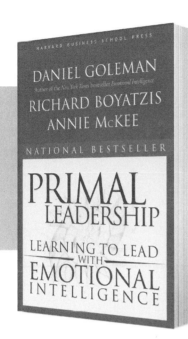
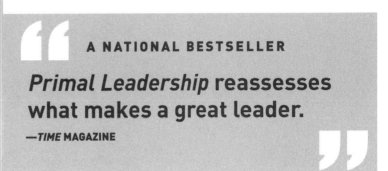
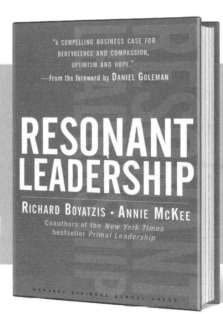